Develop Your Leadership Voice

Speaking with a powerful voice is the backbone of successful leadership. A leader needs their voice to calm people down, reassure people with certainty and hope, foster connection, build trust, convey the vision, inspire teams, and drive results. This book shows you that the voice you were born with can be changed.

Through proven, step-by-step exercises, readers will learn how to:

- Project gravitas and exude executive presence.
- Cut through the noise and command people's attention.
- Convey credibility and certainty through one's voice.
- Project calmness in times of anxiety and panic.
- Speak with passion and conviction to inspire and influence.

Readers will be able to develop a powerful voice that articulates thoughts with power and presence, that cuts through the noise and distractions, that navigates people through uncertainties with ease and hope, that motivates and inspires people through chaotic situations, and that leaves a lasting impact on people and your organisation.

Written by a professional speaker and voice coach, this book gives you the tools to speak and lead with assurance and confidence.

Cynthia Zhai is a voice coach, professional speaker (CSP), and best-selling author. She has coached professionals from 52 countries across six continents to speak with a powerful voice. As a professional speaker, Cynthia has spoken in 24 countries across five continents for the past 23 years.

"Whenever anyone asks me for a voice coach, I recommend Cynthia Zhai. Why? Because I know she will help them develop their voice as a leader and give them practical ways to continue becoming more and more powerful with their public speaking. Now that Cynthia has put her groundbreaking processes in this book, this will become the gift that keeps on giving. If you are a leader or you aspire to be one, this is a must-read. Cynthia is the world's voice coach."

Craig Valentine, *MBA, World Champion of Public Speaking, Author of* World Class Speaking

"Cynthia shared in-depth insights on essential qualities needed in a leader's voice to enhance leadership presence. She guides readers through insights and wisdom on how to liberate your mind and emotions of your voice and offers practical exercises to develop your powerful voice as a leader."

Low Peck Kem, *Chief HR Officer and Advisor (Workforce Development), Singapore Public Service Division, Prime Minister's Office*

"In a time when uncertainty shakes the confidence of teams and leaders alike, Cynthia Zhai delivers a remarkable guide for finding and refining your leadership voice. This book is not just about speaking – it's about inspiring trust, connection, and hope. With a step-by-step approach, Cynthia equips leaders with the tools to project a voice that calms in chaos, reassures in doubt, and motivates with clarity. She also delves deeply into the mental and emotional barriers that hold us back, empowering every reader to grow from within and lead with lasting impact. If you're ready to elevate your influence and create a powerful ripple of positive change, this book is your blueprint."

Ron Kaufman, *Bestselling Author of* Uplifting Service

"In today's labyrinth of relentless change, this book stands out as a beacon for leaders. It equips you with the tools to communicate in a digital world, and to command and inspire confidence among your employees during these transformative times."

Robin Speculand, *Specialist in Strategy and Digital Implementation, Author of* World's Best Bank *and* Implement

"In times of uncertainty, an impactful voice is more than a skill – it's a necessity. Cynthia unveils the secrets to commanding presence, influence, and authenticity through voice mastery. This book goes beyond technique, weaving together mind, heart, and body in a way rarely seen in works on this subject.

In my work in applied psychology, I've come to realize that deepening self-awareness and self-regulation enhances every aspect of life. At its core, it comes down to mastering our mental, emotional, physical, and spiritual intelligence. If this resonates with you, this book is the guide you've been looking for."

Barney Wee, *Research & Development Director, Mind Transformations Pte Ltd*

CYNTHIA ZHAI

Develop Your Leadership Voice

How to Speak with a Powerful Voice That Assures, Unites, and Influences People

Routledge
Taylor & Francis Group
LONDON AND NEW YORK

Designed cover image: Getty images

First published 2026
by Routledge
4 Park Square, Milton Park, Abingdon, Oxon, OX14 4RN

and by Routledge
605 Third Avenue, New York, NY 10158

Routledge is an imprint of the Taylor & Francis Group, an informa business

British Library Cataloguing-in-Publication Data
A catalogue record for this book is available from the British Library

ISBN: 9781032979854 (hbk)
ISBN: 9781032979830 (pbk)
ISBN: 9781003596486 (ebk)

DOI: 10.4324/9781003596486

Typeset in Joanna
by KnowledgeWorks Global Ltd.

Access the Support Material: www.routledge.com/9781032979830

This book is dedicated:

To my parents for their unconditional love that has been and
will be with me for the rest of my life.
To my sisters, who always believe in me and support me,
blindly at times.
To my niece and three nephews, who have inspired me
to love unconditionally.

Contents

Preface

"People hear you on your level of consciousness."

The level of your current personal growth shows up in the way you speak or the way you write. As my level of consciousness advances, so does how the audience receives my messages.

An audience member shared after a speech, "Cynthia, I heard you a few years ago. Both times I've learned so much, but this time, it felt different, in a very good way."

If you read my last book, *Influence through Voice*, published in 2015, you'll see the growth and maturity in this book.

My clients and audiences are my source of inspiration. They keep on pushing the envelope, bringing the same yet different voice problems to me that allow me to dig deeper and create innovative yet effective approaches. You'll see in this book that working on your voice is more than working on the techniques or exercises. It is a holistic process of working on the whole you.

This reminds me of the differences between Western medicine and Chinese medicine. Western medicine focuses on treating specific symptoms by isolating the problem, whereas Chinese medicine focuses on the holistic and overall balance of the body, mind, and spirit. When I examine your voice problems, I don't separate them from the rest of you, with an eye for a quick fix. I look at you as a whole being. Now I sound like a medical doctor. I guess my parents' dream of me becoming a doctor is fulfilled in some sense after all.

The fact is that voice work itself is holistic by nature. For example, breathing is the foundation for a powerful voice. Breath is our life force and reflects how you interact with the world around you. Learning the breathing exercises is one side of the coin, and releasing what keeps you from withholding your breath is the other. It is my responsibility to address them both to solve the problem once and for all.

I hope you'll realise from reading the book that working on your voice is not a matter of learning a tool but rather going through a process of transformation.

Michael Beckwith, new thought minister and best-selling author, once said, "We don't attract what we want. We attract who we are."

Who do you need to become in order to speak with a powerful voice that assures, unites, and influences people?

To transform your voice and move to the next level of your leadership, you must transform who you are so you can match the next level you want to reach.

May this book bring you the answers you have been seeking.

May this book support you in your journey of transformation.

May this book open new doors to your continuous advancement.

Cynthia Zhai

Acknowledgements

I'm blessed to have the support and inspiration of those who have helped me to make this book a reality.

Thank you, Barry Clarke, for showing up at the right time and the right place to introduce me to Taylor & Francis.

Thank you, Kendrick Loo, for recognising the value of the ideas in this book.

Thank you, Chelsea Low, for keeping me on track.

Thank you to all my clients and audiences from around the world, who always remind me to be relevant, inspire me to become more creative, and help me to fulfil my mission and purpose in this life.

Thank you to all my teachers who showed me the way when I felt lost and confused.

Thanks to all those who contributed their perspectives in the surveys during the initial stage of the book: Jens Quedens, Yvonne Zhu, Gerald Blackburn, Erick Lansard, Tse Nan Lim, Andrei Chew, Bas Keijzer, Rachel Won, Richard Chia, Emmanuel Hebe, Najib Abdullah, Wikum Hettiarachchi, Dreamy Somani Shah, Dave Sousa, Geetika Agarwal, Nageswara Nukala, Iman El Noamany, Valentine Low, Livio Deltin, Salman Bokhari, Mohammad Sohfi Abdul Hamid, Julie F, Sjoerd De Clerck, Yeo Poh Sai, Hanny Aguswan, Bhai Mera, and David Liu.

As Helen Keller put it, "Alone we can do so little; together we can do so much." Thank you for being part of my journey.

One

"The ultimate measure of a leader is not where they stand in moments of comfort and convenience but where they stand in times of challenge and controversy."

– Martin Luther King Jr.

THE COMPLEX AND UNCERTAIN TIME WE ARE LIVING IN

"I need to give them hope and reassure them."

"How do I speak to calm them down when we are fighting fire?"

"How can I sound more empathetic when everything needs to move quickly?"

These are questions my clients have asked when they started their first voice coaching session. I'm not surprised by what my clients wanted to achieve – to speak to connect, comfort, and motivate people as a leader, now more than ever.

The world we inhabit today is characterised by unprecedented levels of complexity and uncertainty. From rapid technological advancements to geopolitical shifts, climate change, and economic volatility, the landscape is constantly evolving in ways that challenge our ability to predict and plan for the future.

As a leader, it is imperative to understand the intricacies of this complex and uncertain world and its various dimensions and the implications for individuals, organisations, and societies to help you prepare people to navigate them.

Technological complexity

One of the most significant drivers of complexity is the exponential growth of technology. The digital revolution has transformed virtually every aspect of our lives, from communication and commerce

DOI: 10.4324/9781003596486-1

to healthcare and education. However, this rapid pace of change brings with it a host of challenges:

- Data overload: The sheer volume of data generated daily is overwhelming. Though big data analytics offer powerful insights, managing and interpreting these data effectively is a complex task.
- Cybersecurity threats: As our dependance on technology grows, so does the risk of cyberattacks. Protecting sensitive information and critical infrastructure from malicious actors is a constant battle.
- Ethical dilemmas: Technologies like artificial intelligence (AI) and machine learning raise profound ethical questions. How do we ensure that algorithms are fair and unbiased? Who is responsible when autonomous systems make decisions with significant consequences?

Geopolitical uncertainty

The global political landscape is fraught with uncertainty. Traditional alliances are shifting, new powers are emerging, and conflicts are flaring up in various parts of the world. This geopolitical uncertainty has far-reaching implications:

- Trade wars and economic sanctions: Trade disputes and economic sanctions create uncertainty for businesses, affecting supply chains, market access, and investment decisions.
- Migration and refugee crises: Political instability and conflict drive mass migration, placing significant strain on host countries and challenging international cooperation.
- Climate change and resource scarcity: Climate change intensifies resource scarcity, leading to competition and potential conflict over water, land, and energy resources.

Economic volatility

The global economy is marked by volatility, with fluctuations in financial markets, currency values, and commodity prices. This economic uncertainty affects businesses, governments, and individuals alike:

- Financial instability: Economic crises, such as the 2008 financial meltdown and the COVID-19 pandemic, highlight the fragility of the global financial system.

- Income inequality: Economic volatility often escalates income inequality, with the wealthy able to weather downturns more easily than the poor.
- Job insecurity: Technological automation and global competition are reshaping the job market, leading to job insecurity and the need for continuous re-skilling and up-skilling.

Environmental uncertainty

Climate change is perhaps the most pressing environmental challenge of our time, introducing a high degree of uncertainty:

- Extreme weather events: The frequency and intensity of extreme weather events, such as hurricanes, droughts, and wildfires, are increasing, posing significant risks to communities and infrastructure.
- Biodiversity loss: The rapid loss of biodiversity threatens ecosystems and the services they provide, from food security to clean air and water.
- Policy uncertainty: The lack of consensus and coordinated action on climate change at the international level adds to the uncertainty, making it difficult for businesses and governments to plan for the future.

Social complexity

Societies are becoming increasingly diverse and interconnected, leading to a complex web of social interactions and challenges:

- Demographic shifts: An increase in ageing populations in some regions and youth populations in others presents unique challenges for social services, healthcare, and education.
- Cultural diversity: Increasing cultural diversity requires greater sensitivity and understanding, as well as policies that promote inclusion and integration.
- Social inequality: Persistent social inequalities, including those based on race, gender, and socioeconomic status, create tensions and demand for social justice.

Health and pandemic uncertainty

The COVID-19 pandemic underscored the uncertainty and complexity of global health challenges:

- Emerging diseases: The emergence of new infectious diseases and the resurgence of old ones pose significant threats to public health.

- Healthcare access: Disparities in healthcare access worsen health inequalities, with vulnerable populations often bearing the brunt of disease outbreaks.
- Vaccine development and distribution: The race to develop and distribute vaccines highlights the complexities of global cooperation, supply chain management, and public trust.

The world we live in is undeniably complex and uncertain, shaped by technological advancements, geopolitical shifts, economic volatility, environmental challenges, social diversity, and health crises.

CURRENT WORKFORCE REALITIES

The current complexity and uncertainty in the world have significantly impacted employees in several ways.

Mental health and well-being

One of the most significant impacts has been on employees' mental health and well-being. The constant stream of unsettling news, combined with concerns about job security, health, and economic stability, has led to increased stress and anxiety levels. The blurred lines between work and personal life, a phenomenon aggravated by widespread remote work arrangements, have contributed to higher levels of burnout. Employees often struggle to disconnect from work, leading to longer working hours and an always-on mentality. Furthermore, feelings of isolation and loneliness have become more prevalent, especially for those working remotely, as the spontaneous social interactions and support networks typically found in traditional workplaces have diminished.

Job security and career progression

The current climate has also raised substantial concerns about job security and career progression. Economic downturns and industry-specific struggles have left many employees worried about potential job loss or reduced hours. The uncertainty about career growth opportunities has added to employees' stress, as have concerns about the need to re-skill or up-skill to keep up with technological changes and new job demands. The rapid pace of digital transformation has made it crucial for employees to continuously update their skills, which can be both challenging and overwhelming.

Work–life balance

Maintaining a healthy work–life balance has become increasingly difficult for many employees. Those working from home, caring for children or elderly relatives, or managing additional responsibilities have found it particularly challenging to juggle their professional and personal lives. The lack of physical separation between work and home has made it harder for employees to switch off, leading to increased burnout and decreased overall satisfaction. Moreover, the need to adapt to new work environments, as in remote work or hybrid work models, and new technologies has added to the cognitive load and stress experienced by employees.

Financial stress

Financial stress has also become a significant concern for many employees. Economic uncertainty, inflation, or reduced income have led to worries about future financial security and retirement savings. The instability in the job market and the broader economy has left employees feeling uncertain about their financial futures, contributing to overall anxiety and stress levels.

Adaptation to new work environments

Effective communication and collaboration have also been impacted by the current complexities and uncertainties. In remote or hybrid work settings, maintaining productive and engaging interactions with colleagues has presented challenges. Non-verbal cues and spontaneous conversations, which are crucial for building rapport and fostering collaboration, are often lost in virtual environments. This has made it more difficult for employees to build and maintain professional relationships and networks, which are essential for career growth and job satisfaction.

Decision and change fatigue

The constant need to make decisions and adapt to changes in a complex and uncertain environment has contributed to decision fatigue and change fatigue among employees. The cognitive load required to process vast amounts of information, evaluate risks, and make informed decisions can become overwhelming. This continuous state of adaptation and uncertainty can lead to decreased productivity, increased stress, and a general sense of weariness.

To support employees during these challenging times, it is crucial for leaders to prioritise open communication, address mental health and well-being with empathy, offer flexibility and understanding, and empower employees to adapt to new technologies and job demands, fostering a sense of growth and resilience, so that together you can navigate the complexities and uncertainties more effectively and resiliently.

ESSENTIAL SPEAKING SKILLS FOR LEADERS IN A CHAOTIC WORLD

Effective speaking skills are indispensable for business leaders. The ability to communicate clearly, persuasively, and empathetically can reassure employees, build trust, rally and inspire teams, and help navigate crises with resilience and confidence.

Throughout history, leaders have faced chaotic times that required exceptional speaking skills to inspire, unite, and guide their followers. These leaders have used their oratory prowess to navigate crises, rally support, and bring about significant changes.

Winston Churchill's speeches during World War II are legendary for their ability to galvanise the British people and the Allied forces. In the face of the Nazi threat, Churchill's words were a beacon of hope and determination. His "We Shall Fight on the Beaches" speech, delivered on June 4, 1940, is a prime example of his rhetorical power. Churchill's ability to articulate the gravity of the situation while instilling a sense of resilience and defiance was instrumental in maintaining morale and unity during one of Britain's darkest hours.

Mahatma Gandhi's speeches during India's struggle for independence were a powerful tool in his nonviolent resistance movement. Gandhi's ability to communicate his philosophy of nonviolence and civil disobedience in a clear and compelling manner inspired millions of Indians to join the cause. His speeches were not just about political goals but also about moral and spiritual values, making them resonate deeply with the Indian people. Gandhi's oratory skills were a key factor in mobilising the masses and ultimately achieving India's independence.

Nelson Mandela's speeches during the struggle against apartheid in South Africa were instrumental in rallying support for the anti-apartheid movement. His "I Am Prepared to Die" speech, delivered during his trial in 1964, is a poignant example of his eloquence and conviction. Mandela's words were not just a defence of his actions but a call to action for all those fighting against injustice. After his release from prison, Mandela's speeches continued to inspire people towards reconciliation and unity, culminating in his inaugural address as South Africa's first black president in 1994.

Angela Merkel, the former Chancellor of Germany, is widely regarded as one of the most influential leaders of the modern era. Her speaking skills were instrumental in guiding Germany and the European Union through numerous crises, including the European debt crisis and the refugee crisis. During the refugee crisis in 2015, Merkel's address to the German people was a powerful statement of compassion and responsibility. She famously declared, "*Wir schaffen das*" ("We can do this"), conveying a sense of determination and optimism that resonated with her audience. Merkel's ability to communicate clearly and effectively was a key factor in her successful leadership.

Yuriko Koike, the governor of Tokyo, showed exceptional leadership and communication skills, particularly during the COVID-19 pandemic. Her speeches were marked by a sense of urgency, clarity, and empathy, reflecting her commitment to protecting the health and well-being of Tokyo's residents. Koike's ability to communicate effectively was crucial in implementing measures to control the spread of the virus and providing support to those affected. Her addresses to the public were a source of guidance and reassurance, demonstrating her strong leadership and determination to navigate the city through the crisis.

Leaders throughout history have demonstrated the following essential speaking skills required to thrive in a chaotic world to engage, influence, and inspire.

Clarity and conciseness

In a chaotic world, clarity and conciseness are paramount. Leaders must be able to convey complex ideas in a simple and straightforward manner. Many of my clients whose first language is not English are often concerned that the words they use are too simple. But simplifying language and avoiding complicated words or jargon ensure that the message can be understood by all stakeholders. As teams become increasingly global, most team members will not speak English as their first language either. Clarity and conciseness are crucial for cutting through the noise and being heard in the chaos.

Empathy and emotional intelligence

In difficult times, people need to know that you care. Leaders who can understand and connect with people's emotions are better equipped to inspire and motivate them. Active listening, which involves paying attention to people's needs, concerns, and feedback, demonstrates respect and builds trust. Using empathetic language that acknowledges and validates people's feelings fosters a deeper connection. These skills are essential to be able to comfort, reassure, and motivate people.

Building and maintaining trust

Leaders must provide accurate information and address concerns directly. Transparency is key. Acknowledging what is known and unknown helps to manage expectations and maintain credibility. Leaders should demonstrate a genuine understanding of the audience's needs and concerns, showing that they are actively engaged and committed to finding solutions. By being honest, straightforward, and responsive, leaders can foster a sense of security and trust even in the most turbulent situations.

Adaptability and flexibility

In a chaotic world, leaders must be adaptable and flexible in their communication styles. Tailoring the message to suit different audiences and contexts ensures that the message resonates. Being open to feedback and willing to adjust the message based on the audience's response demonstrates flexibility and responsiveness. The ability to think on one's feet and respond to unexpected questions or situations is essential in a dynamic environment. This adaptability allows leaders to stay relevant and effective, even as circumstances change rapidly.

Engaging and inspiring storytelling

The ability to tell a compelling story is often emphasised by my clients. Storytelling is a powerful tool for engaging the audience and making complex ideas relatable. Leaders who can craft compelling narratives can inspire and motivate their teams. Using personal stories and anecdotes can humanise the message and make it more memorable. Structuring your message as a story helps to capture and maintain the audience's attention. Incorporating emotion into stories makes them more likely to resonate with the audience and inspire action.

Authenticity and integrity

Authenticity and integrity are foundational for building trust and credibility. Leaders who speak from the heart and align their words with their actions are more likely to be believed and followed. Being genuine and speaking honestly and transparently build trust and foster a culture of openness. Ensuring that what is said is consistent with what is done demonstrates integrity and reliability. Acknowledging and taking responsibility for mistakes shows humility and builds trust. Authenticity and integrity are essential for establishing a strong leadership presence and gaining the respect and loyalty of followers.

Crisis communication

The role of crisis communication has been pivotal in recent years. Leaders must be prepared to communicate calmly and effectively during crises to navigate organisations through challenging and unexpected situations. Clear, timely, and accurate communication can calm people down, mitigate panic, maintain trust, and provide much-needed guidance to stakeholders, including employees, customers, and the public. By prioritising transparency, empathy, composure, and consistency in their messaging, leaders can minimise the negative impact of crises, protect their organisations' reputations, and ultimately steer their teams towards recovery and resilience.

Influencing and persuading skills

The ability to influence and persuade is essential for driving change and gaining buy-in. Leaders who can articulate a compelling vision and persuade others to support it are more likely to achieve their goals. In challenging and difficult times, when people are experiencing anxiety and panic, leaders need to persuade and influence them to move forward and take action. Effective influencing and persuading skills enable leaders to overcome resistance, rally support, and drive meaningful change.

Cultural sensitivity

In a globalised world, cultural sensitivity is crucial. The cost is high when leaders fail to recognise this. Leaders must be aware of and respectful of cultural differences to ensure that their messages are well received. Being mindful of cultural norms, values, and communication styles helps to avoid misunderstandings. Using language that is inclusive and respectful of diverse backgrounds fosters a sense of belonging. Adapting one's communication style to suit different cultural contexts ensures that the message is relevant and appropriate. Cultural sensitivity is essential for building bridges, fostering collaboration, and uniting people to foster an inclusive and respectful environment.

Digital communication skills

In an increasingly digital world, leaders must be proficient in using digital communication tools. Being comfortable and effective in delivering presentations via video conferencing and other digital platforms is necessary and especially vital for crisis communication. Using social media to engage with stakeholders and amplify the message can extend the reach and impact of communication. Mastering digital communication skills enables leaders to stay connected, engage with a broader audience, and leverage technology to enhance their communication effectiveness.

Powerful speaking skills are a critical leadership capability in today's complex and chaotic world. Leaders who can communicate clearly, empathetically, and persuasively are better equipped to navigate uncertainty, inspire their teams, and drive positive changes.

SPEAKING SKILLS AS A WHOLE

"Good morning, everyone!"

Victor led a global team focusing on cyber security in financial industry. He needed to speak and present at conferences regularly.

"My content is boring by nature. How can I improve my voice to be more interesting so they won't fall asleep?"

I asked him to give the beginning of his presentation.

"Good morning, everyone. Here's the agenda of my presentation."

I facepalmed, "No matter how interesting your voice is, 'Good morning' won't get them excited about your presentation."

As I looked further through his entire presentation, I noticed it was structured as a textbook:

- Welcome and introduction
- Objectives of the presentation
- Understand cybersecurity
- Best practices
- Conclusion

"With a presentation as this, no wonder they'll fall asleep." We both laughed.

"To grab and keep their attention, you've got to work with how attention functions, not how your logical brain works."

We ended up working on restructuring his presentation first.

"I've got a story."

Lim tried to use a story to motivate her team, "I was told to have stories in my speeches. How do I deliver the story to be engaging and inspiring?"

I looked through her story. It went like this:

"A few years ago, I had X challenge. I was able to overcome the challenge. Here are three lessons I've learned."

"Have you seen any superhero movies?" I asked.

Lim looked puzzled, "Yes?"

"Imagine the Batman movie went like this:

First scene: When I was young, my parents were killed.

Second scene: Now I'm protecting the city from bad people.

Third scene: Dressed up in Batman suit, I'm sharing with you the three lessons I've learned."

We both burst into laughter.

"No matter how dynamic your voice tries to be, the way you tell your story is guaranteed to bore people. No one tells stories in that way!"

We had to work on building the story first.

Another Les Brown

Michael led a project team in a consulting firm. He had a gentle temperament. His voice was soft; he shared, "I'd like to develop a powerful voice to motivate my team."

I asked him to deliver a random speech, and I heard him adopting another voice, "Are you impersonating Les Brown?" (Les Brown is a motivational speaker.)

"How do you know?! He's my favourite speaker."

"He has a distinctive voice." I laughed, "You and he have very different personalities. You can't just mimic a voice that you like. You are you. We need to find YOUR distinctive voice."

We spent some time in understanding who he was and what personality he had before trying to figure out what his distinctive and powerful voice was.

To speak to influence and inspire, you can't just work on one area – for example, your voice – while leaving other areas to fall short; it is a complete package.

One of the most cited studies on effective speaking is the model proposed by Albert Mehrabian in the 1960s [1]. In his research, he found that the impact of a message is conveyed 55% through body language, 38% through voice, and 7% through words. Though his research was conducted with a small sample and within a specific context [2], it offered valuable insights into the importance of all three key elements of communication.

Speaking skills encompass a combination of several key elements, voice, body language, what you say (such as word choice, content, structure), audience engagement, your unique speaking style, etc. Each of the elements plays an indispensable role in speaking to be heard, influence, and inspire.

In the following chapters, our key focus is on your voice. We'll also cover other elements as necessary. All the elements work together as a whole.

REFERENCES

[1] Mehrabian, A. (1967). "Inference of Attitudes from Nonverbal Communication in Two Channels." *Journal of Consulting Psychology*, 31(3), 248–252.

[2] Lapakko, D. (1997). "A Reexamination of Mehrabian's Verbal and Nonverbal Communication Research." *Journal of Business Communication*, 34(4), 429–443.

What makes a powerful leadership voice

Two

"Words mean more than what is set down on paper. It takes the human voice to infuse them with deeper meaning."

– Maya Angelou

WHY ARE YOU NOT BEING HEARD?

> **"That idiot was promoted."**
>
> Alan has been passed over for promotion to be senior vice president at work, "I am as competent as the other candidate. Just because he speaks better. I actually did more work. Sometimes I found the work he did was so substandard. It's not fair. What can I say? That idiot was promoted."
>
> In weekly meetings, Lyla often found that her suggestions fell on deaf ears. A few moments later, another person would bring up the same idea and be given the credit. She was the one who had the idea in the first place! She was also frustrated that she often got cut off when she spoke. Most people don't see her as a leader but see her as a specialist in a certain area; for example, a researcher or an analyst.
>
> Vincent noticed after he finished speaking that people often had no response or gave him an indifferent look. Then someone else in the meeting would say the exact same words and get people nodding or responding.

Do you find yourself in similar situations? You worry that you'll be stuck in the same position, feeling trapped and stagnant. You start to question your capabilities and your confidence decreases. You become concerned with your career prospects and financial stability.

You've heard people say, "It is not what you say but how you say it that matters." It is more than how you say it that matters. How you say

DOI: 10.4324/9781003596486-2

it often refers to how you structure your thoughts and construct your sentences, which is important. But the predicament my clients often face is the lack of ability to speak with a voice that can capture people's attention, make people look up and listen, have their message heard and leave a strong impact.

What is it in your voice that stops you from being heard? Here are three major reasons.

1. Your voice is too small.
   A powerful leadership voice gives people the impression that it's "big." It is not loud. In fact, being loud is the wrong way to project your voice.

   When you speak, your voice is projected in a limited space. It doesn't travel far or wide. It could be that your voice is too soft or you are mumbling or your pace is too fast.

   Another often overlooked voice problem is that of holding your voice back. This is different from a soft voice or mumbling. It's the projection stuck in the mouth, as if you were talking to yourself, murmuring. Many clients with this voice problem often find people asking them to repeat themselves or saying that they sounded aloof.
2. Your voice lacks gravitas.
   Gravitas in a person's voice refers to the sense of weight, seriousness, or authority that it conveys. It's a quality that commands attention and respect, making others more likely to listen to and consider what you are saying. This is what most clients are looking for in developing their leadership voice.

   A voice that lacks gravitas could be too high-pitched, too fast-paced, or just in general unable to carry weight. This often gets worse when one is nervous or stressed that the voice starts to tremble and become high-pitched or one starts speaking too fast.
3. Your voice leaves no impact.
   When you speak, whether in meetings or presentations, people don't have much opportunity to respond to what you say in the moment. You have no idea whether your message is getting across. Sometimes you might see people yawning as you speak. You may find it challenging to grab and keep people's attention. You may wonder if it's because your voice is monotonous and too boring. That will affect your confidence and often you will try to speed up your talk to finish quickly, which reinforces a lack of impact.

Your voice is more than a tool to convey information. Voice work is more than working on the tone of your voice. As a leader, your voice is a powerful tool to engage and connect with people, command attention and respect, instil trust, establish your authority, and motivate people towards action. Unfortunately, many leaders overlook the power in their voices and miss the opportunity to connect with people on a deeper level and to truly influence and inspire people.

Most people don't like the sound of their own recorded voice. The fact is that this is the voice others hear. I often joke with clients, "Don't be embarrassed. You are the only one who hasn't heard your voice." To know how you sound to others, and of course to improve, you have to listen to your own voice. The good news is that you can change the voice that you were born with. You don't have to live with a voice that makes you cringe every time you listen to it. The hidden potentials in your voice carry the power to transform your experience with your own voice and your impact on the people around you.

How clients have changed after working on their voices

Briana was seen as an inexperienced leader when new people joined her team. When she spoke, her words didn't seem to have much impact on the new team members. She was disappointed that her voice didn't reflect her expertise and competency. She wondered whether it was because she had difficulty communicating in an interesting way, thus leaving people feeling uninfluenced and uninspired. After working together for a few months, she was surprised at the transformation in her voice, and even more surprised at the responses from her team members: "Now they just go and do what I have instructed without any doubt or argument. That's probably what we meant by 'authority' in my voice!"

Chris had a "small" voice that often got talked over in meetings. In cross-function meetings, his opinions were never heard. Though sometimes he expressed his views, people seemed to forget: "Chris, you haven't shared." Over time, he started to feel anxious in meetings, worrying that people would think he was not as competent. As we worked on his voice, he started to experience a stronger projection. People started to look up when he spoke. When he didn't speak, people were waiting to see what he had to say, as if his words would reassure them. "This is unbelievable." Chris shared at our last coaching session,

"I had never thought this was possible. I'm feeling more and more confident as a leader."

Nelson started to film videos and podcasts as his marketing initiatives to establish himself as a thought leader in his field of expertise. He didn't like to hear his own voice. "I sound like an ordinary Joe." He rolled his eyes, "It doesn't project any authority or thought leadership."

"Perhaps a normal Nelson," I joked.

"I would love to have a voice like Morgan Freeman's. It sounds so trustworthy and authoritative, yet pleasant!"

"Let's help you develop those qualities in your voice then," I replied.

When we were finishing our work together, he was very happy to report, "I recorded some new videos lately and I LOVE my transformed voice!"

VOICE QUALITIES FOR POWERFUL LEADERS

What makes a powerful leadership voice?

Nelson was not alone. Many clients want to have a voice like Morgan Freeman's! Well, some want Sean Connery's. "Whatever Morgan Freeman sells, I'll just buy!" one client shared.The qualities that clients appreciated in Morgan Freeman's voice include trustworthy, credible, authoritative, humble, pleasant to listen to, deep, relaxed, and calm.

For female clients, the range is more diverse, and voices that are liked most include Oprah Winfrey's, Michelle Obama's, Angela Merkel's, and Michelle Yeoh's. The most important qualities they appreciated are empathetic, calm, trustworthy, and firm.

Throughout history, leaders who drove change and left a lasting impact also demonstrated the voice qualities that make a powerful leader.

Winston Churchill's speeches, such as "Never Give In," "Blood, Toil, Tears and Sweat," and "We Shall Fight on the Beaches," were all marked as determined, reassuring, and commanding and successfully rallied British people together during the darkest hours of World War II.

Martin Luther King Jr., with his iconic "I Have a Dream" speech, used his resonant, melodic, and emotive voice to advocate for civil rights and inspire movement.

Mahatma Gandhi, though soft-spoken, was able to carry profound clarity and conviction in his speeches on nonviolence and Indian independence. His calm yet firm voice resonated deeply with his followers.

Lee Kuan Yew, Singapore founding prime minister, was renowned for his distinctive speaking style and voice, which were characterised as direct, assertive, authoritative, emotionally expressive, and well-paced. His exceptional speaking skills played a pivotal role in transforming Singapore from a struggling third-world country into a thriving first-world nation.

Aung San Suu Kyi, Myanmar democracy icon and Nobel Peace Prize laureate, speaks with a voice that has a unique blend of strength, authority, and warmth. Her voice was instrumental in her leadership and advocacy for democracy and human rights and in her ability to inspire and mobile people both in Myanmar and around the world. When she spoke, it was not just with words but with a reflection of her vision, values, and unwavering commitment to justice and freedom.

Germany's former chancellor, Angela Merkel, speaks with a voice that's calm, steady, and authoritative and conveys both confidence and reassurance, marking her as one of the most influential leaders of the 21st century who earned respect and admiration both at home and abroad.

New Zealand's former prime minister, Jacinda Ardern, has a voice that's known for its warmth, empathy, and strength. The speeches she delivered during times of crisis combined strength with compassion, making her a beacon of leadership and hope and a role model, especially for young women.

It's not hard to see what common voice qualities people are looking for in leaders, especially in the current world with rapid technological change, global interconnectivity, and increasing demands for social responsibility and ethical behaviour.

Trustworthiness

With fake news, misinformation, and polarising narratives prevalent today, trust in leaders plays a vital role and shapes their ability to inspire, influence, and drive change, and it is a critical factor in the success of their organisations [1].

How you as a leader speak, with a voice that conveys trust so that people follow your guidance, feel assured, and take action, is of utmost importance.

Authenticity

With the erosion of public trust, the rise of social media, and the increasing number of youth in the workforce, people value leaders who are honest, transparent, and genuine.

Ironically, authenticity can't be faked. This is just common sense. When you have the slightest inauthenticity, it'll show up in your voice. Voice reflects everything about you and in you. When you develop authenticity in your voice, you will be developed as a leader who's authentic.

Compassion

In recent years of crisis and with the ongoing rapid pace of change, compassionate leadership is of increasing importance. Employees look to their leaders for support, empathy, and guidance to help them navigate uncertainty and manage stress.

Compassionate leaders are believed to inspire higher levels of loyalty and commitment from their employees, leading to improved performance and reduced turnover [2].

It's not enough for leaders to feel compassionate in their hearts while speaking in a monotone. People won't be able to feel that. You need to let people feel that you care when you speak, in conjunction with the actions you take.

Composure and certainty

The world is changing at an accelerated rate, combined with several major crises in recent years such as the COVID-19 pandemic, economic downturns, and natural disasters, which can lead to anxiety and panic. The focus on mental health has been brought to the forefront over the past few years. It is in times of uncertainty that people look to leaders who can stay calm and grounded, provide certainty, and inspire hope.

It is your words, delivered through your voice, that make a difference. Does your voice soothe people, calm them, and give them assurance and hope? Or does it make the situation worse? Your voice should reflect your composure and certainty when you want to encourage and inspire people.

Conviction

In the face of chaos and crisis, leaders need to have strong convictions to make decisive choices. Even when no one knows when the uncertainty will end, leaders can reassure people that "we'll get through this" and help people move forward. A leader's conviction gives people a sense of direction and purpose, providing stability, resolve, and resilience in the face of challenges. It helps leaders to inspire trust, foster unity, and make progress.

Conviction is not merely in the head. It must resonate deeply in the heart and body. You can't just know the conviction in your head – you must express the conviction through your voice.

WHAT TO DEVELOP IN YOUR VOICE TO SPEAK AS A POWERFUL LEADER

What is NOT a powerful voice?

A powerful voice is not a loud voice. Many people consider having a loud voice as one that is able to project and that shows confidence and authority.

Loudness is the result of improper voice projection. Loudness has a higher pitch that is not comfortable to the ears and can be perceived as aggressive, intimidating, and overpowering. Clients who spoke with a loud voice were frustrated with the negative perceptions: "People around me say that I sound aggressive." When people have that perception of you, they'll drift away from you, shut down, or go against you, rather than taking action. Your message is not heard.

A loud voice can also stem from passive aggression or a sense of losing or lacking control. Regardless, you will not be heard.

A loud voice may be the armour that you build around yourself to make you look and sound strong so no one will dare to get close to you, take advantage of you, or defeat you. Unfortunately, keeping up this facade is exhausting, and it's not where the real power comes from. The real power comes from a place within you that's grounded, centred, and unwavering. When you speak from that place, you will be empowered and empowering.

Following are the areas you want to develop in your voice to be powerful.

Space

A powerful voice is not loud but "big." It takes up space. It has nothing to do with how big or how small your physical size is. It has to do with how you project your voice. A voice that takes up space draws attention and makes you more noticeable. People look up when you speak and are encouraged to listen more attentively. You are more likely to be perceived as a leader or influential figure.

Presence

You have a vocal presence as much as a physical presence. Most people place emphasis on building up their physical presence, their posture, or appearance and overlook the vocal presence. You can have the most powerful physical presence, with the potential to impress and inspire, yet the moment you start speaking, if your voice trembles or sounds like "Mickie Mouse," no one will listen, regardless of your powerful physical appearance. The incongruence between your physical presence and vocal presence works against you. People will lose their trust and confidence in your ability to lead.

Gravitas

As discussed earlier, *gravitas* refers to the sense of weight, seriousness, or authority a person's voice conveys. Many leaders came to me wanting to develop gravitas in their voice. "It somehow commands attention and respect. It has the magic of being seen as a leader." Leaders who speak with gravitas convey trust and certainty. People feel reassured and calm around them. Gravitas is not guaranteed through a lower pitch. It is the result of full resonance, which you'll learn in later chapters.

Depth

A deep voice is often associated with authority and leadership. Leaders with deeper voices have an unfair advantage. This is true for both men and women [3, 4]. A deep voice is NOT a low voice or, to be more specific, a low-pitched voice. Many people try to lower their voices by pressing the vocal cords down to sound more authoritative or credible. That is the wrong way to project your voice and a good way to damage your voice. A deep voice is three-dimensional. It has depth and width. It is the result of proper projection and full resonance, which you'll learn in later chapters.

Emotion

Emotion is a key driver of inspiration and motivation. Without it, your words will fall flat and fail to move people to action. Emotions help you as a leader build connection and trust, express empathy and compassion, and drive change and transformation with conviction. Genuine emotions in leaders are a sign of authenticity. Speaking without emotion can come across as preoccupied, uninterested, and disengaged, as well as insincere, inauthentic, and apathetic.

Speaking with emotion is not about becoming emotional, which can be overwhelming to both you and others. It is about expressing your emotions genuinely and appropriately. Even when you don't express emotions verbally, your body language and actions indicate emotional cues.

Equanimity

Equanimity is the ability to stay grounded and centred regardless of what's happening externally. Even when the world around you is challenging and chaotic, one can remain calm and composed. Equanimity is the internal unshakable and unwavering centre that you draw your strength and power from. It is the centre of a tornado: calm, peaceful, and still. When you operate from that place, your power and impact are beyond measure. Equanimity in leaders is especially valuable in today's turbulent and volatile external environment.

A voice projected from a place of equanimity calms people in the midst of chaos and uncertainty, reassures them, and inspires them to move forward.

YOUR UNIQUELY POWERFUL VOICE – YOUR SIGNATURE VOICE

Everyone's voice is unique. Voice is vibration and very susceptible to what happens in you. Your voice has infused everything about you since you were born, where you were born, how you have grown up, what you have been through, what you are going through, what is stuck in you mentally and emotionally, what is holding you back psychologically, and much more. Your voice reflects everything about you. Your voice is indeed your identity. You will find no one else with the same exact voice as yours in the world. It is like your fingerprint – your voice print.

Developing a powerful voice with the qualities above is not a cookie-cutter process. Your powerful voice is unique. It amplifies the positive qualities you have and elevates you to the next level of yourself, someone who has the power to influence and inspire people around you. You'll feel more empowered to be who you are.

REALITY CHECK

1. Do you often get talked over in meetings?
2. Do you find it difficult to jump into a discussion?
3. Do people have no or little response after you speak?

4. Does someone else share the same idea and have a better response and impact?
5. Does what you say often get ignored in meetings?
6. Are you often asked to repeat yourself?
7. Do people not see your competence and experience the first time they hear you speak?
8. Does your energy drop after speaking for some time?
9. Does people's attention drift after hearing you speak for some time?
10. Does your voice tremble or become high-pitched or fast-paced when you get nervous or emotional?
11. Do you have difficulty projecting your voice far and wide?
12. Do you seldom think about how people feel after hearing you speak?
13. Have you ever purposely lowered your voice to sound more executive like?
14. Do you find it's hard to maintain a powerful voice?
15. Do you think you need to pause more strategically when you speak?
16. Do you find people have no "wow" response the moment you start speaking?

If you answered "yes" to more than three of these questions, let's get to work!

REFERENCES

[1] Edelman. (2023). Edelman Trust Barometer. https://www.edelman.com/trust/trust-barometer

[2] Boyatzis, R. E., Smith, M. L., and Blaize, N. D. (2012). "Developing Sustainable Leaders through Coaching and Compassion." *Academy of Management Learning & Education*, 11(1), 88–106.

[3] Mayew, W. J., Parsons, C. A., and Venkatachalam, M. (2013). "Voice Pitch and the Labor Market Success of Male Chief Executive Officers." *Evolution & Human Behavior*, 34(4), 243–248.

[4] Anderson, R. C., and Klofstad, C. A. (2012). "Preference for Leaders with Masculine Voices Holds in the Case of Feminine Leadership Roles." *PLoS ONE*, 7(12), e51216. doi:10.1371/journal.pone.0051216

Leadership voice quality – Space

Three

"Take up space. Make noise. Sing your song. This is your birthright. This is your journey."

– Glennon Doyle

Executive presence is what most clients are looking to develop.

"I've worked on my physical presence but still find something's missing," Luc shared.

"Yes, your voice is not taking up space," I shared.

"What does that mean?"

WHAT IS A VOICE THAT TAKES UP SPACE?

A powerful voice takes up space. It travels far. Many clients say, "I want to be able to throw my voice to the back of the room." "Throwing" your voice is not technically correct. Projection, "traveling," or "carrying" is a more accurate description.

Taking up space also means your voice can project wide. A powerful voice that takes up space is very much like a stereo sound system that envelops your listeners and fills up the space you are in. Clients who have successfully transformed their voices are often surprised yet satisfied with recordings of their new voices: "It's like I have an in-built speaker in my body."

A voice that takes up space captivates people and exudes a certain aura that makes you come off as having a "big" presence. As one client put it, "The moment I speak, I want people to look up and go 'wow'!" That's what a voice that takes up space can help you achieve.

WHAT HELPS A VOICE TAKE UP SPACE

A voice that travels far and wide does not have much to do with your physical stature. It doesn't matter how big or small your physical size is. Audiences around the world are often surprised at how powerful my projection can be, and I am not very big.

DOI: 10.4324/9781003596486-3

Some people often say to me, "Oh, I have no problem projecting my voice. I'm loud." A loud voice is not a voice that takes up space. Loudness has a higher pitch and is not pleasant to the ears. Loudness can also come across as aggressive, instead of a charismatic executive presence, which is what most clients want to achieve. Loudness is the result of improper projection. Over time, speaking with a loud voice will damage your vocal cords.

To understand what helps your voice take up space, you'll first need to understand how your voice is being produced.

The nature of our voice is vibration. Vibration comes from the vocal cords, which are soft tissues (mucous membranes), located in the voice box (larynx). Vocal cords will not vibrate when there is no air – that is, breath – passing through. When breathing out, air passes through the vocal cords and makes them vibrate. That's the source of our voice. The sound vibration is amplified by the sound chambers (also known as resonators, which are cavities) in our body, such as the nose, mouth, throat, voice box, and chest. Then the sound vibration comes through the articulators, including the lips, the teeth, and the tip of the tongue, to help us pronounce different words.

Breath is what powers the vocal cords to vibrate. Breath is therefore the power of our voice. The quality of your voice will never exceed the quality of your breath. If your voice is weak, you need to work on your

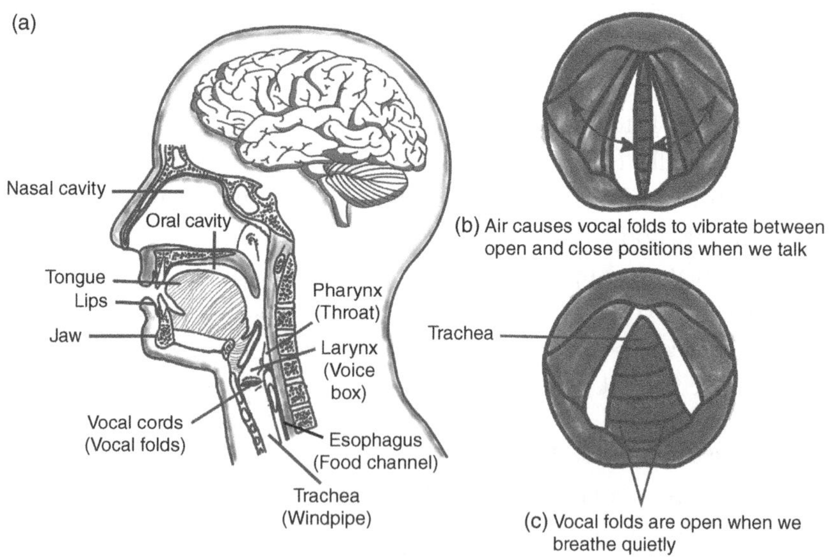

Figure 3.1 Illustration of voice production.

breath. If you run out of breath easily while speaking, you need to work on your breath. If your voice trembles when you are nervous, you need to work on your breath. If you want to improve your voice at all, you must work on improving your breath.

What will help your voice take up space?

1. Your breath.
    - First, breathe properly.
    - What is proper breathing? We will discuss this in the next section.
    - Next, make proper breathing a habit.
    - This is the most overlooked step. Most people think that once you practice proper breathing, your voice will be improved automatically. Proper breathing is not a magic wand. This may sound silly. Though my clients are highly intelligent, I have to reinforce how important it is that you must make proper breathing a habit. That comes with daily practice to re-train how your body works.
    - Third, use proper breath to support your voice projection.

    This is the second most overlooked step. Proper breathing practice by itself does not lead to proper projection. You have to learn and train your body for proper projection to occur.

    What is proper projection? This will also be discussed in the next section.
2. Your physical state.

    That is, whether you are relaxed or tense physically.

    The best voice comes from the most relaxed body. Voice is vibration. Vibration is very susceptible to tension in the body.

    What happens when you are nervous? Your legs shake, your palms sweat, your brain goes blank, your throat feels tight, and your voice trembles.

    Recall times when you felt stressed. How did your body react, and where in your body were you tense?

    In our fast-paced life, most people seldom pay attention to the tension in their body until the tension becomes pain that is hard to ignore.

    Your voice won't take up space if your body is tense. You'll have to learn how to relax so your voice can come out easily and freely.

Stuck in a Cage

Cathy had a harsh-sounding voice, and it didn't embody the executive qualities she wanted. Sometimes it felt like a knife cutting through her throat. It was not surprising that her staff was afraid of her. She was frustrated, "Even when I'm in the other room, they get jitters hearing me speak."

The most challenging hurdle in working with her voice was to get her to relax. Her entire body was too stiff, as if it had been stuck in a cage and it had no room to stretch. What was worse: "You put yourself in this cage," I shared with her.

"How?" She was perplexed.

"You have a structure for everything. Everything needs to be a certain way. Everything is in a cage, and this cage is made of steel that it's too hard to break." I sighed. Talking about it made me feel tense and tired.

"Yes, I'm often said to be stubborn," Cathy responded.

"It's more than that," I smiled. "You are one hard steel that's impossible to break. To take up more space with your voice, you have to break this steel cage that you set up for yourself."

We ended up spending time first on relaxing her body and breaking free from the cage.

You may not be as stiff and rigid as Cathy was. Or maybe you are. We are living in a highly competitive and stressful world. Where does all the stress go? It stays in our bodies as dis-ease. What's in the mind is reflected in the body. It would be shocking if someone had no tension at all in their body. To take up space through your voice, you must first break free from the tension that you've built up in yourself as dis-ease.

BREAK FREE FROM DIS-EASE

Do you experience stiff neck and shoulders, back pain, tight jaw, migraine headache, leg and knee issues, and more?

These are not simply due to poor posture or injury. Nothing is accidental. An apparent physical injury at a specific location in the body is often the culmination of issues that have accumulated there over time.

American neuroscientist Dr. Candace Pert [1] has proven that neuropeptides, or chemical messengers, triggered by emotions, are thoughts converted into matter. Our emotions reside physically in our bodies and interact with our cells and tissues. When you focus on a particular thought, neuropeptides are released and travel to specific locations in the body. If you persist in that thought for an extended period, it may eventually manifest as physical discomfort or pain.

For example, when you are nervous or fearful, your stomach tightens, your heart rate increases, your palms feel wet, your legs shake, your breath becomes shallow, and your voice trembles. Imagine someone who lives in fear most of the time. What physical issues would this person tend to develop? Stomach issues – for example, indigestion – are common [2].

Here's another example. When you are angry, your breath becomes fast and shallow, your face turns red, your heart races, your blood pressure escalates, and your body may even shake or tremble. There is a proven link between frequent anger and high blood pressure [3].

If you experience chronic discomfort, pain, or dis-ease at any certain location in your body, besides consulting with a medical professional, you can discover what possible mental and emotional reasons that have contributed to the dis-ease and therefore heal with a more holistic approach. Among the many books available on this subject is *You Can Heal Your Life* by Louise Hay [4], which focuses on the mind–body connection and the power of affirmations to promote healing. In the book, Louise Hay associates various physical ailments with specific emotional or mental patterns.

Physical issues related to voice projection include regular coughing that is unrelated to a cold or flu, chronic sore throat not attributed to prolonged speaking, or a constant need to clear the throat. According to Lousie Hay, throat issues are often associated with the following emotional or mental states:

- Expression and communication: Throat problems are often associated with difficulties in expressing oneself or communicating effectively. This can include feeling unable to speak up for oneself, suppressing emotions, or feeling like one's voice is not heard or valued.
- Fear of speaking out: Throat issues may be related to a fear of expressing one's truth or opinions. This could stem from past experiences in which speaking out led to negative consequences or judgements.

- Creativity and self-expression: The throat is also seen as a centre for creativity and self-expression. Blockages or issues in this area might indicate a struggle with expressing one's creative energies or authentic self.
- Anger and resentment: Suppressed anger or resentment can also manifest as throat problems. Holding back angry words or feelings can create tension and discomfort in the throat.

Bodily tension affects your voice projection. If your neck and shoulders are stiff, your voice won't vibrate at its best frequency. If your chest is tight and your back hurts, you won't breathe fully and your voice won't be in its most powerful state.

Sometimes clients say, "Tension is good. It makes me focus." That's the type of focus experienced when we are in "fight-or-flight" mode, a reaction that's triggered when we perceive a threat, physical or psychological. It's a survival mechanism that prepares our body to either defend itself or run away. Tension is the result of a reactive response and, if prolonged, is not healthy physically or psychologically. It can lead to chronic stress, which is linked to various health issues, such as anxiety disorder, panic attacks, muscle tension, a weakened immune system, and more. Being relaxed and centred is what we want to achieve. Remember, the best voice comes from the most relaxed body.

It is necessary to work holistically and examine physical, mental, and emotional issues so the result you are working towards – a voice that takes up space – is long-lasting.

Body scan and relaxation

This exercise takes no more than 10 minutes and is a great way to start your day.

Find a comfortable position to sit or lie down. Close your eyes and use your breath to bring consciousness to your body. Using your mind's eye, perform a mental scan of your body from head to toe, relaxing each part as you go.

Use your mind's eye to focus on your head, including your scalp, your ears, your forehead, your face, your eyes, your nose, and your mouth. Is there any tension, discomfort, or pain? Where is the pain? With every breath you take in, visualise your breath traveling to the painful area, and as you breathe out, imagine the pain gradually dissipating and leaving your body.

Continue with your breath and move on to your throat, neck, voice box, and shoulders. Notice whether there is any stiffness, discomfort, or pain in these areas. Locate the stiffness or pain. Inhale to the area and exhale the stiffness and pain.

Move on to your chest, upper back, middle back, lower back, stomach, and belly. If you find any tension or pain, inhale to those areas and exhale the tension and pain.

Continue with your mind's eye and scan your pelvic area, buttocks, thighs, calves, and feet. Is there tension or pain in those areas? If so, focusing on one area at a time, inhale to the painful area and exhale, visualising the pain leaving your body.

Finally, examine your arms, wrists, and hands. Inhale to the tense and painful area and exhale, imagining the pain gradually dissipating and leaving your body.

Once you finish the scan, focus on your belly area and notice the movement with every breath for a minute or two. When you feel relaxed and ready, slowly open your eyes.

Follow the audio guidance for this exercise here: http://developyourleadershipvoice.com/exercises

This is an exercise for temporary relief. For chronic pain and physical issues, you may want to consult a doctor and seek holistic healing, including psychotherapy if needed. I recommend attending self-development programs on a regular basis. We are always a work in progress. We are never done unless we are dead.

ARE YOU BREATHING PROPERLY?

Most people take their breath for granted. They do not pay attention to their breath until they become breathless or when they are nervous and realise that deep-breathing is not helping them to calm down.

Breath is our life force. If you were unable to breathe for 30 to 60 seconds, you would start to lose consciousness. Brain damage would follow in another 2 to 3 minutes without oxygen. Your life would be at an end if the lack of oxygen continued for another 2 to 4 minutes [5–7].

Breath is associated with how we take in and give out life. It symbolises your right to take up space or to retreat from it. Breathing problems are often related to fear or refusal to take in life fully, not feeling worthy to take up space or even exist. Asthma, or restricted breathing, is linked to a feeling of not having the right to breathe for yourself or a feeling of not being able to express yourself fully [4].

Breath is the power of your voice. To speak up for yourself fully and take up space with your voice, you must work on your breathing.

Most people do not breathe properly and have potential for improvement not only in breathing but also in voice and in quality of life in general.

Here's a quick exercise to find out if you are breathing properly. Stand in front of a mirror. Take a deep breath. Notice how your body is moving. If your shoulders go up, your chest moves forward, and your abdomen pulls inward while inhaling and while exhaling your shoulders drop, your chest pulls backward, and your abdomen pushes forward, you are not breathing properly. You may have been breathing in that way for as long as you can remember, but that is not proper breathing.

WHAT'S PROPER BREATHING?

In proper breathing, your shoulders and chest do not move while inhaling and exhaling. Your abdomen moves outward when inhaling and inward when exhaling, the exact opposite movement to the improper breathing that you have been doing.

What happens in the body during proper breathing?

You may have heard people talk about the diaphragm when it comes to breathing or heard someone say, "Breathe from the diaphragm." There's no such thing as "breathe from the diaphragm." The diaphragm is a large, dome-shaped muscle that separates the chest cavity from the abdominal cavity. We don't breathe from the diaphragm. We breathe from the lungs and with the support of the diaphragm.

In proper breathing, when we inhale, the diaphragm moves downward and outward. As a result, the abdomen moves outward. The air goes through the nose or mouth and travels to the lungs through the windpipe (trachea). When we exhale, the diaphragm moves back; that is, upward and inward. As a result, the abdomen moves inward. The air is expelled from the lungs, travels through the windpipe, and leaves the body through the nose or mouth.

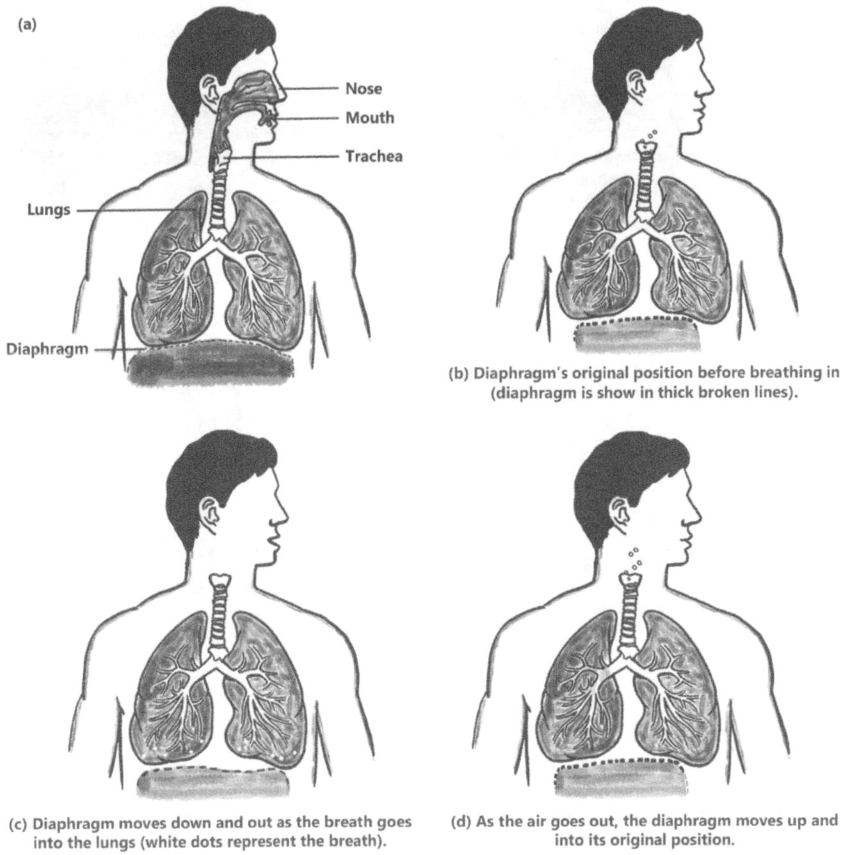

(b) Diaphragm's original position before breathing in (diaphragm is show in thick broken lines).

(c) Diaphragm moves down and out as the breath goes into the lungs (white dots represent the breath).

(d) As the air goes out, the diaphragm moves up and into its original position.

Figure 3.2 Illustration of proper breathing.

When you breathe improperly as described above, you are also using the diaphragm, but your diaphragm is moving in the opposite direction to that in the proper breathing, causing your lungs to compress. You are actually not inhaling more air but less. That's why when you are nervous and breathing improperly, no matter how many deep breaths you try to take, your body does not feel relaxed. Furthermore, when you inhale improperly, your body is contracting and causing more tension. In improper breathing, you may actually feel more relaxed when you exhale as your diaphragm relaxes downward and outward, creating space in your body, with your shoulders dropped and chest downward.

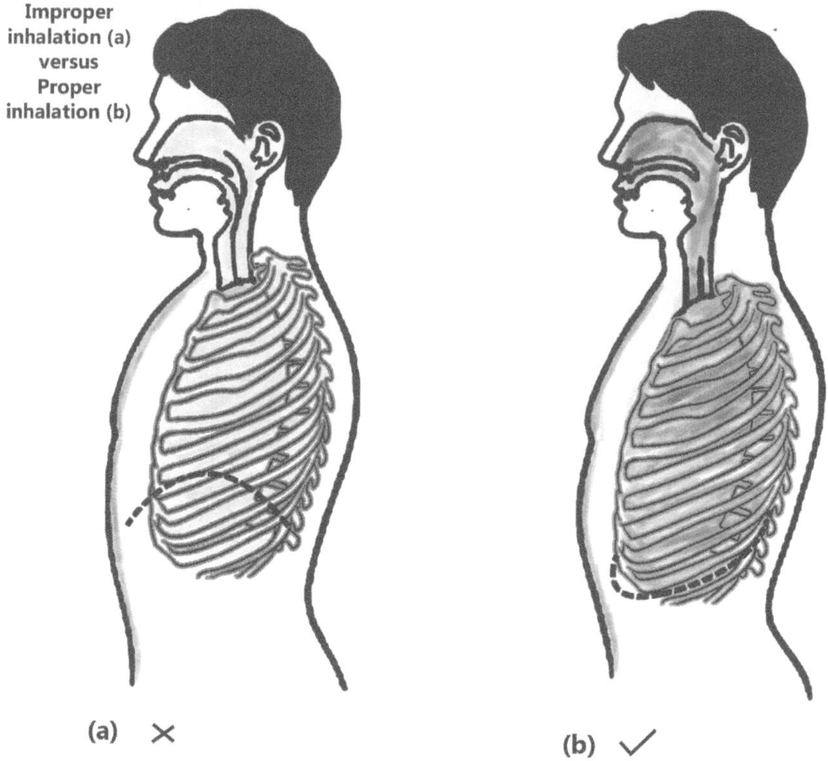

Figure 3.3 Illustration of improper inhalation versus proper inhalation.

BENEFITS OF PROPER BREATHING

The fact is that you should feel relaxed when you breathe in, not when you breathe out. When you inhale properly, your body expands outward, drawing more air into your lungs. The oxygen-rich blood is then transported from the lungs to the heart and the heart pumps this oxygenated blood to the rest of the body through the arteries. You'll feel more relaxed and grounded and be able to think more clearly.

"I can think more clearly now."

Karl was in his mid-50s. He wanted to speak with a stronger voice. His breath was very shallow and his voice was weak. Every day, after the air-conditioner went off in the office at 6 pm, he would have to go outside to get fresh air. Otherwise, in his words, "My mind was foggy, and I couldn't think well."

We first worked on developing his proper breath and made it into a habit. Two months later, he happily reported, "This is surprising. Now I don't have the need to leave the building for air after the aircon is off. I can think more clearly."

"I can lift more weight and run longer."

Waylon wanted to develop a more powerful voice. Though he worked out regularly, he was not breathing properly. As he developed proper breathing into a habit, he shared, "The other day at the gym, I noticed I was able to lift more weight and wasn't feeling tired. That's interesting. I can even run for a longer duration."

That's a very common discovery for many clients who run regularly. They can run for a longer duration without feeling tired or breathless. This makes perfect sense when proper breathing has become a habit.

When you breathe properly, you breathe in more air and use your entire lung capacity, especially the middle to lower part of your lungs. Each breath promotes better oxygen exchange in your body, which helps improve endurance and reduce fatigue [8].

Proper breathing as a habit offers a wide range of health benefits, in addition to improving your voice. Improved lung function can help manage symptoms of respiratory conditions such as asthma and chronic obstructive pulmonary disease (COPD), reduce breathlessness, and help you breathe more efficiently and easily [9, 10]. However, it is important to consult with a healthcare provider before starting any new breathing exercise, especially if you have a respiratory condition like asthma.

Diaphragmatic breathing stimulates the parasympathetic nervous system, which is responsible for the body's "rest and digest" functions, and lower cortisol levels, the body's primary stress hormone, helping to reduce stress and promote relaxation [11].

"I was not breathing!"

After the first coaching session in which we had talked about proper breathing, a client began to become more aware of her breathing. She shared during the second session, "I was at my laptop writing an email. I was quite stressed at what I was about to write, and all of a sudden I noticed I was not breathing! I believe that had happened a lot to me." She paused, "Now I am more conscious and can take a proper breath to relax myself."

"It's great that you have this awareness now," I replied. "Learning starts from awareness."

With your body more relaxed and stress levels lowered, your blood pressure also lowers and your heart rate variability improves [12]. Some clients also found they fell asleep faster once proper breathing has become a habit. Indeed, research shows that regular practice of diaphragmatic breathing can help reduce symptoms of insomnia and improve sleep quality [13].

In all practices that focus on mindfulness, breath has always been a cornerstone. Diaphragmatic breathing helps induce a state of calmness and relaxation, enhance mental clarity, and elevate emotional well-being.

Spiritual practices across various traditions also recognise and emphasise the power of breath for spiritual advancement, aiming to cultivate a deeper connection with the self, the world, and the divine. In Hinduism and yoga philosophy, breath is known as *prana*, the life force or vital energy. *Pranayama* as breath control regulates the breath to promote physical health, mental clarity, and spiritual growth.

In Buddhism, *anapanasati*, mindfulness of the breath, is a foundational practice. It involves focusing the mind on the sensation of the breath as it moves in and out of the body. This practice helps to cultivate concentration, calmness, and insight into the nature of the mind and reality.

In Taoism, breath is *qi* (chi), the vital energy that flows through the body. Qigong practices involve coordinated breathing exercises, movements, and mental focus to cultivate and balance *qi*, promoting health, longevity, and spiritual development.

In Sufism (Islamic Mysticism), breath control is sometimes used in conjunction with the remembrance of God (Dhikr) to induce spiritual states and purify the heart. Certain Sufi orders employ specific breathing techniques during their rituals and meditations to deepen connection with the divine.

Native American and many other Indigenous cultures incorporate breath work into their spiritual practices, often as part of ceremonies, rituals, and healing practices. Breath is seen as a connection to the spirit world and the natural environment, and breathing techniques are used to enhance awareness, intuition, and healing.

Though breath work is not as central to Christian mysticism as it is in other traditions, it does play a role in certain contemplative practices. For example, the Jesus Prayer ("Lord Jesus Christ, Son of God, have mercy on me, a sinner") can be synchronised with the breath [14]. Centring prayer, a contemporary Christian practice, uses a sacred word or phrase repeated internally in rhythm with the breath to quiet the mind and open the heart to divine presence [15]. In Christian theology, breath is often associated with the Holy Spirit (e.g., John 20:22, where Jesus breathes on his disciples and says, "Receive the Holy Spirit").

PROPER BREATHING EXERCISES

One misconception that people often have is that if you practice diaphragmatic breathing when you are nervous, all your voice problems will disappear. However, there's no magic wand for this. Diaphragmatic breathing must become a habit before it can solve many of your voice problems. That means every breath you take in the future should be proper breathing: when inhaling, your abdomen will move outward while your shoulders and chest remain still and when exhaling, your abdomen will move inward while your shoulders and chest remain still.

Another misconception most people have is that they believe that if they practise daily, proper breathing will automatically become a habit. I've had clients who were yoga teachers and, surprisingly, proper breathing was not a habit even though they practice and teach proper breathing regularly. You'll need to progressively practice different levels of breathing exercises to form a habit.

Though you may have heard that it takes 21 days to form a habit, based on the experiences with my clients, developing proper breathing as a habit comes with daily routine practice – for those who practice yoga regularly and those who play wind instruments such as saxophone, trumpet, or flute, it takes about 1½ months. Otherwise, it can take 2 to 3 months.

Here are two steps of breathing practice to help you make proper breathing a habit.

Step 1: Kung fu breathing exercises

Exercise 1: Single Kung fu

Sit or stand comfortably. Lying down is not recommended as your first option for practice because we don't spend most of our time lying down in bed, unless movement of you abdomen is stiff when practising while sitting or standing upright.

Place your hand on your stomach where your diaphragm is located. Inhale. If your first inhalation is not proper, that's fine. We'll start with correcting your exhalation.

Now with some air in your lungs, push your entire abdomen inward and allow the air to come out through your mouth. If you did that with ease and comfort, you have completed a proper exhalation. You should feel an urge to take a breath in and the abdomen will automatically move outward. This is considered one set. Repeat the process a few more times.

Exercise 2: Double Kung fu

The only difference with this exercise is that when you breathe out, instead of pushing your abdomen inward once to empty all the air, you'll push the abdomen inward twice in one breath; that is, two folds. Each fold is distributed evenly with half of the breath.

This exercise is extremely helpful for those whose abdominal movement is stiff.

The exercises are demonstrated in videos in the course listed on the website: http://developyourleadershipvoice.com/courses.

In these exercises, in step 1 and step 2 you'll breathe through the mouth. This helps your facial muscles relax, and makes it easier for the air to go in and out. It also works as a reminder to move your abdomen properly while forming this new habit. You'll be able to breathe through the nose automatically when proper breathing has become a habit.

Practice either or both of the exercises for 1 to 1½ months daily. The body needs regular stimulation to be reprogrammed. You can practice as many times as possible every day, each time for 2 to 3 minutes.

Most people who do not breathe properly have difficulty moving their diaphragm in the right direction. Intentional exercises train your diaphragm to do that. You'll need to perform these exercises for 1 to 2 months to train your diaphragm, as well as your body, to move properly. Learning proper breathing is a process of re-training or re-conditioning your diaphragm and your body. It is not a one-off activity. Without re-conditioning, your body and your voice won't be able to remain calm and composed when you are nervous, stressed, or emotional.

"Nothing is changed."

Lisa's voice sounded young and immature. She wasn't getting the recognition she felt she deserved at work. In the first session when we worked on proper breathing, Lisa shared that she had very shallow breath and she often felt breathless while speaking. When she came back for the second session 2 weeks later, she was frustrated. "This is not working. I still have shallow breath. Nothing is changed, neither my breath nor my voice!"

"Of course nothing is changed." I laughed, "This is not a magical pill that you take and everything starts working. How I wish that to happen to you. Your diaphragm and your body have been working in the wrong way for years. It takes time to re-condition it. Even to tone your muscles, you need time to see the results. It's not like you go to the gym once and you have a six pack."

Over the next few sessions, Lisa was able to understand how the body worked in forming habits. Interestingly, she also started to see how the corporate culture had trained her to be impatient and too result focused. Sometimes, counterintuitively, going slow is the best way to go fast. Take your time to form a habit in the beginning. Once the habit is formed, you'll never need to do any exercises, and your breath and your voice will be changed – for good.

What to look for in Kung fu breathing practices:

- Are you feeling relaxed before, during, and after the practice?
  If not, something in your practice is not correct. If your abdomen feels tired, you might have contracted your muscle instead of pushing it in with ease. When contracting your abdomen, you'll notice that your whole upper body moves instead of staying still and the movement of the abdomen is very limited.

  Our respiratory system is a flawless mechanism that can take care of itself. That is, when you push your abdomen in with ease, the air should automatically be expelled from your lungs due to the upward and inward movement of your diaphragm. It's not by you trying to control how every part of your body moves. Your body will get out of sync when you do that. All you need is one action: pushing your abdomen in with ease while opening your mouth so the air can come out.

This requires you to relax your mind and let your body lead. Interestingly, the more intelligent my clients are, the more slowly they progress, because they are trying to use their mind to control how the body works. Relax your mind, let go of your attempt to control, and trust that your body knows what it's doing. The more attuned you are to your body, the faster you'll progress and the more relaxed you'll feel before, during, and after practising.

Some clients take longer time to form a habit of proper breathing. They need to unlearn, tearing down the existing building to create space for something new to be built. It is not a process of fixing something here and there in the old mental building you already have. You've heard the saying "old habits die hard." What's stopping you from adopting a new habit is your tight grasp on the old pattern, something familiar and safe. To master something new, you have to let go of the old. Empty your glass before pouring a new drink.

- Is your abdominal movement obvious?

The objective in Kung fu breathing is to re-train how your diaphragm works. When the abdominal movement is not obvious or too little or too subtle, it does not have much effect on re-training the diaphragm. One side-benefit is that when the abdomen moves outward more, it draws more air into your lungs and utilises the entire lung capacity you have. Over time, your lung capacity will increase, which will help you with your stamina and bring a multitude of health benefits, as mentioned earlier.

Many female clients are concerned with obvious movement of the abdomen. Remember, this is only for practice. When proper breathing becomes a habit, the abdominal movement is more subtle.

- Does your abdomen move with ease and flexibility?

If your abdominal movement is abrupt and tense, you are not practising properly. It might be that you are only contracting or squeezing the muscle. The abdomen is flexible, as if it were elastic, easily moving in and out with every exhalation and inhalation.

If you have difficulty moving the abdomen with ease and flexibility, try practicing the panting exercise described next.

Panting for abdominal movement with ease and flexibility

Place your hand on your stomach. Focus on moving your abdomen in and out rapidly. You'll notice that your breath and the movement of your abdomen are in sync. That is, when your abdomen moves inward, you are breathing out; when your abdomen moves outward, you are breathing in. Practice the exercise for a few minutes and stop when you start to feel light-headed.

You may feel light-headed during Kung fu breathing practices as well. That is normal at first. When that happens, slow down to rest.

You feel light-headed is owing to hyperventilation. As you breathe deeply or rapidly, you are exhaling more carbon dioxide than usual. This can lead to a decrease in the level of carbon dioxide in your blood, a condition known as hypocapnia. Hypocapnia can cause the blood vessels in your brain to narrow, reducing blood flow and leading to symptoms like light-headedness and tingling or numbness in the extremities. Though less common, it's also possible that you are not inhaling enough oxygen while practising breathing exercises, leading to a state of low oxygen in your body, resulting in dizziness. The symptoms can usually be relieved by slowing down your breathing. If the symptoms persist, they may be due to other underlying health issues, in which case you may wish to consult with a healthcare professional [16].

How do you know if your practice is correct?

1. Your body is relaxed, not tense or tired anywhere. If your abdomen feels tired, as mentioned earlier, you are likely squeezing or contracting your abdominal muscle.
2. You don't experience dry mouth or dry throat. If you do, you might have sucked the air in when inhaling. Relax and allow the air to flow in.
3. Your abdomen moves with ease and flexibility.
4. You feel air/breath pass by your vocal cords and throat effortlessly. There should be no intentional effort used on your vocal cords.
5. You feel that the breath comes out of somewhere deeper in the body – to be exact, the bottom of your lungs – when exhaling.

In summary, the objective in the breathing exercises is to re-train and re-condition your diaphragm and your body to breathe properly.

To achieve that, the abdomen must move easily, flexibly, and obviously. Only then can you move on to the next step breathing exercise.

Step 2: Slow breathing exercise

Sit or stand comfortably. Place your hand on your stomach where the diaphragm is located. Do a few single Kung fu or double Kung fu exercises. Then on an exhalation, move your entire abdomen inward slowly and continuously for a count of 5, followed by an immediate inhalation. Allow the air to flow in and out through your mouth. Repeat the process a few more times.

This exercise gets closer to normal breathing. It is to further re-train your diaphragm to breathe properly. Check the same five criteria above to know whether your practice is correct. This exercise can now replace the Kung fu breathing exercises. You can practice as many times as possible every day for 2 to 3 minutes each time. After 1 to 1½ months of practice, you should notice that your normal breathing is changed to proper breathing; that is, diaphragmatic breathing.

That is how change happens in your breathing. Most clients wonder whether they have to do something different with their normal breathing during the first 2 to 3 months of practicing steps 1 and 2. "How will my normal breathing change if I don't do anything?" The good news is that in your daily normal breathing, you don't need to do anything. But every day you need to re-train your body and your diaphragm by doing the breathing exercises. That's all you need to do. Once the body is trained, you will breathe properly as a habit. Some clients have been surprised at the change: "This is like magic. My normal breathing has changed."

With proper breathing now a habit, some clients noticed that their voice sounded more relaxed and stronger or that their speaking rate was slower, and their overall stamina has improved.

USE PROPER BREATH TO TAKE UP SPACE

"They said that I sounded aloof."

Jay wrote to me before our first meeting: "I have a soft voice and people often ask me to repeat myself." When I met him in person, I realised the problem was not that he had a soft voice. The problem was that when he spoke, he held his breath. As a result, his voice appeared to be small, not taking up any space, which was in contrast to his physical height of 1.9 meters (6.2 feet).

"When you hold your breath to speak, it can come across as unclear and uninterested in what people are saying," I shared with him.

"No wonder my staff said I sounded aloof," Jay realized. "Sometimes they said I appeared as if I did not want to listen but wanted them to finish what they had to say quickly, and there were times that I did think they needed to quickly finish talking and get back to work!"

"Ha-ha!" I laughed, "And that thought you had, unfortunately, showed up in your voice."

When we speak, we are supposed to breathe out. It is the out breath that powers the vocal cords to vibrate and generate sound in the first place, followed by resonance, supplementary vibration, in the sound chambers/cavities/resonators such as the nose, mouth, throat, etc.

The problem for most people is not that they try to speak when inhaling, which is not possible. The problem is that most people try to speak while holding their breath. That has happened to almost every client. You may think that that's not the case for you. However, it might have happened when you were nervous or when you were talking with someone who's more authoritative. These are the situations my clients have reported where they've caught themselves holding their breath and trying to speak at the same time.

When this occurs, you'll notice that your voice sounds soft, you speak quickly, and you speak in a monotone. After a while, you feel breathless. People listening to you may have the impression that you don't sound confident, credible, or powerful.

To take up space with your voice, you must use your proper breath while speaking. You'll sound much more powerful.

To use your proper breath while speaking, first you need to become aware of when you are holding your breath. When you notice you are holding your breath, don't take another breath, which is what most people think they should do. You need to first release the breath you are holding. Most people think, "Ah, it's to pause to release the breath and then breathe in." That can work. But in the middle of speaking, you don't want to pause unintentionally, which may seem weird and too deliberate. Instead, find a word to release the breath on.

For example, "The best voice comes from the most relaxed body." Let's say you are too nervous when you start saying this sentence and are holding your breath. Halfway through the sentence, after the word "most," you realise the issue. Instead of pausing to breathe out and then breathe in, you'll release the held breath on the word "relaxed." It looks something like this:

The best voice comes from the most rela ... xed body. You will release the held breath as you say the syllable "la." This is not to elongate the syllable but to use all the held breath to propel the sound. Most clients found this difficult and didn't know how to manage the breath; that is, the sound and the breath out on the sound. Remember that voice is generated automatically when you release the breath because that's how sound is produced without your intervention. You don't have to purposely do anything. What you need to do is to breathe out all the held breath and say the second syllable as you proceed with the sentence. If it's still challenging, try saying the second syllable while sighing.

Most clients asked, "I'm reading a sentence. I know what words are coming up, so I can prepare. Does this apply in daily normal speaking?"

Yes. You don't have to know the script to prepare anything. As you speak, whenever you realise you are holding your breath, the next word will be the word you release the held breath on.

If it doesn't come easily with this exercise, I recommend that you practise for 5 minutes every day. Think of anything that you often need to say at work and use that as your practice material. It requires practice before it becomes easy and looks effortless.

"When do I have to breathe in after I've released the breath?" This is another frequently asked question. When you are speaking, you don't want to have too many things to think about: "I need to release the breath. Now I need to breathe in. Where should I breathe in? What's my message again?"

As much as we think we can multi-task, we perform the best when we are laser focused on one single task. Focus on when you need to release the held breath and release *all* the breath. When you have released all the breath, your body will prompt you to take another inhalation automatically. If you don't feel the urge to take another breath in, you haven't released *all* the breath.

CHARACTER DEVELOPMENT FOR TAKING UP SPACE

Over the years, clients have told me, "I have developed my voice and now it's stronger. I still felt something's missing comparing to your voice."

I've also noticed that even after they have developed their powerful voice, something's still holding some clients back that resulted in them not speaking up in meetings or showing the audience who they are. Some major mental and emotional blocks that were holding them back from taking up space include the following

- Fear of being visible
- Fear of being judged
- Fear of criticism
- Fear of rejection
- Fear of making mistakes
- Fear of inadequacy
- Fear of not being liked
- Fear of social isolation
- Fear of confrontation
- Fear of being exposed as weak/vulnerability
- Fear of authority
- Fear of uncertainty
- Fear of losing control

We'll dive deep into the major fears and talk about the others in the following chapters.

Most clients have replied, "Oh, I don't have fears. It's stress." You might want to work on the fear of vulnerability if you think the same. Stress is a type of fear. Love and fear are two primary emotions, and all emotions can be traced back to love or fear [17].

Fear of being visible

"You haven't introduced yourself!"

Norah was attending a board meeting as a member of a newly formed board. The chairperson asked everyone to introduce themselves. Norah started the ball rolling. "Since I wanted to be seen, I thought I'd start first," Norah shared with me when recalling the story.

After one round of introduction, the chairperson turned to her, "Oh, you haven't introduced yourself!"

Norah was frustrated. "I was the first person who did that." She shared, "There it was again. No one heard me!"

Some clients are introverts and don't want to draw attention to themselves. Visibility makes them feel uncomfortable. Unfortunately, visibility is vital to your career and business growth. To see is to believe. If people don't see you speak up, how can they believe that you are capable? No wonder you get passed over for promotion. Over time, this erodes your confidence and leads to a cycle of self-doubt and resentment: "How could that idiot get promoted and not me? I'm more capable."

The fear of visibility is the discomfort or anxiety that people experience when they feel exposed, noticed, or scrutinised by others. This can come from early childhood experiences, past negative experiences, or cultural and societal norms where standing out is discouraged.

Fear of being judged

Almost everyone has this fear, "What will they think of me?" We are often concerned with how people perceive us, and it can manifest in various ways, from mild anxiety to severe avoidance behaviours.

The fear of judgement is the anticipation of negative evaluation. We worry that others will criticise, ridicule, or reject us based on our actions, appearances, or opinions. This often begins with early life experiences. Children who grow up in environments where they are frequently criticised or where high expectations are placed on them may develop a heightened sensitivity to judgement.

The fear of judgement can limit your personal and professional growth. When it comes to speaking up and taking up space, it can prevent you from expressing your true self, instead holding back your thoughts and feelings, leading to a lack of authenticity and intimacy in your interactions with people, let alone impact.

Fear of making mistakes

"I'm a perfectionist." Many clients would agree. This results in the fear of making mistakes when speaking or taking too long to craft your sentences or find the right word. This can make you nervous and you may indeed make a mistake, which makes you more nervous until eventually you decide not to speak up.

The fear of making mistakes can be paralysing. It is your anticipation of a negative outcome. You are worried that the mistakes will lead to criticism or a loss of respect from others. This fear can originate from early childhood and past experiences, and it prevents you from speaking up. You may not be very good at speaking on the spot. You may need a lot of time to prepare what you want to say or prefer to read from a script when making a presentation. You may lament, "I need to be even better prepared." No, you are already best prepared. It is your fear of making mistakes that is the problem. As a result, you lose the connection with people. You are too much in your head and you cannot take up space.

Fear of inadequacy

Most of my clients are high performers, and many believe that they are "not good enough." At its core, this fear is the perception of not measuring up, of not meeting the expectations of others or even one's own standards. You may worry that you lack the skills, knowledge, or qualities needed to succeed, especially in competitive environments such as today's workplaces.

The fear of inadequacy has its roots in early childhood or past experiences where you were criticised, compared to others, or held to unrealistically high standards. Today's competitive working environment does not help. This fear often leads to self-criticism and avoidance: "I don't know well yet to speak up" or "I don't deserve to take up space yet." You might shy away from further leadership roles or opportunities, fearing that your perceived inadequacies will be exposed, which can also lead to another fear – the fear of being a fraud.

Fear of not being liked

The fear of not being liked originates from the fundamental human need for acceptance and belonging, driving people to seek approval and validation outside of themselves. When this need is not met, it can lead to a persistent anxiety about how one is perceived, creating a cycle of self-doubt and insecurity.

This fear has its roots in early life experiences. Children who grow up in environments where they are often ignored or made to feel unimportant tend to develop a fear of not being liked or accepted.

As a result of this fear, you may not speak up or take up space, worrying that this will not be well received by others, leading to a constant preoccupation of pleasing people around you. Over time, you'll become frustrated and resentful of not being able to express your true self, pursue what you really want, or take up a leadership role.

Fear of confrontation

The fear of confrontation comes from a desire to avoid disagreement, conflict, tension, and the potential negative consequences that may arise from addressing issues directly. As a result, you may agree with others even when you disagree, suppress your own needs and desires to keep the peace, or sidestep important discussions to maintain peace.

Growing up in environments where conflict was handled poorly, where expressing disagreement was met with punishment or disapproval, or where harmony was prioritised above all else can instil a deep-seated aversion to confrontation.

The fear of confrontation prevents you from expressing your true needs and feelings, leading to a buildup of resentment, unresolved issues, and passive-aggressive behaviours.

Fear of authority

The fear of authority is characterised by a sense of anxiety when interacting with or challenging those in positions of power or influence. It can be traced back to early life experiences such as growing up in environments where authority figures were strict, punitive, or unapproachable. Cultural and societal norms in which hierarchical structures are emphasised and questioning those in power is discouraged can also contribute to this fear.

This fear prevents you from advocating for yourself, expressing your own opinions, or taking on leadership roles. You will not speak up even when you have valuable insights to share or take up space in fear of the potential backlash from superiors.

WORK THROUGH THE FEARS

I am not a believer in "Feel the fear and do it anyway." Fear is a profound and deep-seated emotion that needs to be unpacked, understood, and unraveled.

Here's a process that has worked for me and many clients. If your situation is more serious, or if you want to address the fears with more depth and develop coping strategies, you may wish to seek professional help such as psychotherapy.

Go through each of the fears you have with the following process. As you read through the major fears, understand that fears are formed over time, with ingrained beliefs. Take your time to work through them, but stick with the practice. I'll see you on the other side.

Release your fear

Dedicate a notebook for this exercise and come back to review for progress.

Step 1: Acknowledge your fears

Recognising and acknowledging your fears is the first step to overcoming them. Most people are not aware that they are affected by fear, or they try to deny it as stress. Fear is a screaming child that asks for attention. If you don't acknowledge it, it'll cry louder and louder. When fear is not acknowledged, you are led by it, dragged around, living in reactive mode with continuous anxiety. To release your fears, you need to become the master of your fears.

Which fear do you want to work on when it comes to speaking up and taking up space?

Write it down in your notebook. If you have many fears, write them all down but circle one to work on at a time.

Step 2: Find the source

Fears have their roots in early life experiences. The environment and culture you grew up in have a profound impact in shaping who you are, your fears, your beliefs, your perceptions, etc.

Write down your answers to the following questions:

What were your parents like when you grew up; that is, their personalities?

How did they encourage or discourage you?

Did they compare you with other kids?

How did your birth order affect your experience?

What was your family dynamic like growing up, among your parents, your siblings, if any, and you?

Did cultural or societal norms have an impact on the fear?

Did any other significant life event contribute to the fear?

Now that you've reflected on your early life experiences, how did this fear come about?

Step 3: Challenge your negative thought patterns

Your upbringing and significant life events have shaped your beliefs that caused the fear. For example, being visible means danger; making mistakes means you'll lose respect from others; not being liked means you'll be all alone.

What are your negative thought patterns on your fear? Write them down and see how you can reframe them. For example, "Making mistakes means I'm a human being and it makes me approachable."

My fear of visibility

Having been raised by a dominant parent, my father, who's volatile and has unpredictable temper, I had learned to be invisible around him and at home. That survival strategy didn't serve me later on in my career, however. In fact, it was my biggest stumbling block to career advancement and I had to learn the hard way.

I realised that to me being visible meant being in danger of being criticised and physically hurt. I reframed it as "being visible so I can reach out and support more people." That new belief helped me to make breakthroughs in my career. People often say to me, "I see you everywhere." I'm comfortable with being seen. Visibility has established me as a person of influence in my field and among my peers. Most importantly, it has helped me to support more people around the world.

Step 4: Reveal your hidden beliefs

What beliefs do you have related to what you fear?

For example, if you have a fear of authority, the beliefs around authority could include authorities are intimidating; authorities are hypocrites; authorities are ruthless; authorities are cold-blooded; authorities don't smile much; and so on.

If you fear being visible, the beliefs around visibility could include people who are visible are arrogant; people who are visible have no substance; people who are visible are attention-seekers; etc.

If you see people in authority as hypocrites, subconsciously you don't want to release the fear. Once you take up space and become a person of influence, you wouldn't want people to think of you as a hypocrite.

If you see people who are visible as arrogant, subconsciously you'll sabotage every effort you make to be visible, because you don't want to be seen as arrogant. We can't deny the fact that some people who are visible may appear arrogant, but there are many who don't.

Write down all your beliefs related to what you fear so you will not sabotage your efforts to overcome the fear.

Step 5: Imagine the worst scenarios

We don't fear the fear itself but the consequences and repercussions that come with it.

What's the worst that would happen to you if your fear came true?

Write down all the possible negative consequences you can think of.

For example, if you have a fear of making mistakes, what would happen if you did make a mistake? The consequences could include people will laugh at me; my boss will never trust me; I will lose money; no one will hire me; with no income I will become homeless (the ultimate worst scenario for a lot of people); etc.

Step 6: Use your logic

Has each of the worst scenarios you've listed above ever happened to you?

If your answer is "no," what are you worrying about?

If your answer is "yes," write down the answers to the following question: Did you manage to come out of the worst scenario that happened to you? If you are kicking and alive, then you have come out of that!

This step helps you realise that even if your fear came true, you could handle it.

Step 7: Take small steps

Expose yourself to situations that trigger your fear. Make a commitment to take one small step at a time.

For example, it could be commenting on what someone said at a meeting; asking a question at every meeting; standing up whenever you speak to your team so you can be seen more and take up more space; or starting to list the major points instead of using a script. Get creative in figuring out the smallest step you could take.

It goes without saying that to release your fear takes regular practice so your internal beliefs and thought patterns can be changed and replaced. Leaders who take up invisible space have worked on themselves and embodied the qualities people admire, such as stepping up, courageous, determined, not afraid of being judged or criticised, not going after popularity, not afraid of confrontation, authentically expressing their true self, and more.

That's what you can and will develop.

REFERENCES

[1] Pert, C. B. (1997). *Molecules of Emotion: The Science Behind Mind–Body Medicine*. Scribner.

[2] Mayer, E. A. (2000). "The Neurobiology of Stress and Gastrointestinal Disease." *Gut*, 47(6), 861–869.

[3] Siegman, A. W., Townsend, S. S., Civelek, A. C., and Blumenthal, J. A. (2000). "Anger Expression and Blood Pressure Reactivity during Interpersonal Conflict." *Health Psychology*, 19(5), 429–437.

[4] Hay, L. (1984). *You Can Heal Your Life*. Hay House.

[5] Hornbein, T. F. (2006). "Hypoxia and the Brain: A Brief Review." *Journal of Experimental Biology*, 209(17), 3175–3185.

[6] Wijdicks, E. F. (2001). "The Clinical Diagnosis of Brain Death." *New England Journal of Medicine*, 344(16), 1215–1221.

[7] Bruce, D. A., and Baudry, M. (1995). "Hypoxia-Induced Loss of Consciousness: A Review." *Aviation, Space, and Environmental Medicine*, 66(5), 423–431.

[8] Hopkins, S. R., and Waggener, T. B. (1989). "Effect of Respiratory Muscle Training on Exercise Performance in Healthy Individuals." *Sports Medicine*, 8(6), 341–354.

[9] Mehra, Y. R., Ağaçkiran, M., Akgün, Z., and Kalpaklıoğlu, F. (2007). "Effect of Diaphragmatic Breathing on Lung Function and Exercise Capacity in Asthma Patients." *Respiratory Care*, 52(1), 62–68.

[10] Gosselink, R., Decramer, M., Demedts, M., Troosters, T., and Verschakelen, J. (2011). "Breathing Exercises for Chronic Obstructive Pulmonary Disease." *Cochrane Database of Systematic Reviews*, 4.

[11] Ma, X., Yue, Z. Q., Gong, Z. Q., Zhang, H., et al. (2017). "The Effect of Diaphragmatic Breathing on Attention, Negative Affect and Stress in Healthy Adults." *Frontiers in Psychology*, 8, 874.

[12] Joseph, C. N., Porta, C., Casucci, G., Casiraghi, N., Maffeis, M., et al. (2005). "Slow Breathing Improves Arterial Baroreflex Sensitivity and Decreases Blood Pressure in Essential Hypertension." *Hypertension*, 46(4), 714–718.

[13] Tsai, H. J., and Chen, J. L. (2010). "Effectiveness of Paced Breathing for Insomnia: A Meta-Analysis." *Behavioral Sleep Medicine*, 8(1), 24–34.

[14] Anon. (1930). *The Way of a Pilgrim*. R. M. French, Trans.

[15] Keating, T. (2006). *Open Mind, Open Heart*. Bloomsbury Academic.

[16] U.S. National Library of Medicine. (2024). "Hyperventilation." https://medlineplus.gov/ency/article/003071.htm

[17] Jampolsky, G. G. (2019). *Love Is Letting Go of Fear*. Beyond Words.

Leadership voice quality – Gravitas

Four

"Leadership is not about being liked, it's about being respected. And respect comes from seriousness, not silliness."

– Simon Sinek

Many clients want to develop *gravitas* in their voices: the quality that brings weight to what they say, the quality that commands respect from people, and the quality that leaves an impact.

WHAT IS GRAVITAS?

Gravitas was one of the eight ancient Roman virtues, together with *pietas*, *severitas*, *gloria*, *simplicitas*, *integritas*, *dignitas*, and *virtus* [1].

Gravitas is denoted as "seriousness" and translated variously as weight, dignity, and importance. It is particularly appreciated as an ideal characteristic in leaders [1].

According to the Roman emperor and philosopher Marcus Aurelius, the cultivation of gravitas involves acting with sincerity and dignity, by being temperate in manner and speech as well as by carrying oneself with authority [1].

Cicero, the Roman statesman and philosopher, frequently discussed gravitas in his writings. For Cicero, gravitas was a key component of rhetoric and public speaking, because it conveys a sense of authority and credibility [2].

Over time, gravitas has evolved to describe the demeanour of leaders, public figures, and professionals who carry themselves with a sense of authority and responsibility. In modern days, gravitas is used to describe a person's ability to command respect and attention through their seriousness, dignity, and authority. It is often applied to leaders, politicians, and professionals who exude a sense of importance and credibility.

Many clients who wanted to develop gravitas in their voices have shared:

> "I think when I have gravitas in my voice, I'll be able to command attention and respect."

DOI: 10.4324/9781003596486-4

"Gravitas will help me to carry weight in my words."

"I believe gravitas will help me to convey certainty and credibility as a leader."

"If I have gravitas in my voice, it'll help people to believe in what I say."

"Gravitas gives me the impression that the leader is composed even under pressure."

"We want someone who exudes presence and authority."

Lee was competing for a top leadership role in his company. In the end, Lee didn't get the role. His boss shared with him afterwards, "Even though you have strong technical skills, you are lacking gravitas. We don't see you as a leader who exudes presence and authority. We want someone whom we trust as being able to handle complex situations and various stakeholders well. We do want to grow so you are prepared for the next opportunity. One of the key issues is your voice. It doesn't carry impact." So there Lee was – ready to work with me and acquire gravitas in his voice.

Gravitas has been associated with leadership effectiveness and impact. Leaders with gravitas are considered as exuding authority and carrying themselves with certainty, credibility, trustworthiness, authority, and composure.

Lee was not alone in his failure to get the top leadership role. Many clients have had similar experiences. During executive selections, companies focus on candidates who can speak with authority, whose words carry weight and impact, who command respect from various stakeholders, who are sought after for opinions, and who can remain composed and navigate their employees through complex environments.

GRAVITAS VERSUS PRESENCE

Gravitas

Gravitas is a quality that conveys weight, seriousness, and importance. It's about the substance and depth that a leader brings to their role and interactions. Gravitas is often associated with wisdom, experience, and a certain level of formality or dignity. It's the leader's ability to convey the significance of a situation, to instil a sense of importance and urgency in others and have others take them seriously.

Leaders with gravitas are often seen as thoughtful, deliberate, and authoritative. They speak with conviction and carry a sense of responsibility and consequence. Their words and actions hold weight and influence others. Gravitas is particularly important in high-stakes situations, during crises, or when dealing with difficult decisions. It's about being grounded, steadfast and resolute in the face of challenges.

Presence

Presence, on the other hand, is about being fully engaged and connected in the moment. It's a leader's ability to create a connection and inspire others. Presence is more about the leader's energy, charisma, and ability to engage and resonate with others. It's about how they make others feel when they're with them.

Leaders with a strong presence are often seen as confident, approachable, and inspiring. They have a way of drawing others in, making them feel valued and heard, and creating a positive and energising atmosphere. Presence is about being mindful, aware, and responsive to the needs of the situation and the people involved. It's about being authentic, genuine, and approachable.

"Be here now." In your voice development, when proper breathing becomes a habit, it will help you to cultivate presence as a leader. Another area that'll help you cultivate presence is working on authentic emotions, which we'll discuss in Chapter 5.

Both gravitas and presence are important in effective leadership. Gravitas helps leaders convey the significance of their message and the seriousness of their intent. Presence helps leaders connect with others, build trust, and inspire action. The best leaders know how to balance and blend these qualities to suit the needs of the situation and their audience. They can be serious and authoritative when they need to be but also engaging, inspiring, and present in their interactions with others.

HOW IS GRAVITAS MANIFESTED?

Gravitas is something that can be seen, heard, and felt.

When a leader has gravitas, it shows up in the way they carry themselves; in the way they speak that gives weight to their words; in their voice, which makes people stop and listen and projects certainty, credibility, and authority; and in the trust that people feel towards them, that makes people turn to them for insights and advice, especially in times of chaos and uncertainty.

Gravitas is manifested through non-verbal and verbal communication. That is, your appearance, your body language, your voice, and what you say, including the words, structure, and content. Gravitas is also manifested through your impact.

Gravitas is a manifestation of your innate qualities; for example, your self-awareness, self-acceptance, self-assurance, confidence, certainty, capabilities, and so on.

In this chapter, we focus on developing gravitas through your voice.

"It's not what you say, but how you say it." This is not entirely true. "How you say it" refers to the tone that you use to deliver what you say. Developing gravitas goes further than the tone of your voice.

It is not only what you say but also the voice that you use to deliver what you say. When we say "the voice," it includes more than the tone, pauses, or pacing. It includes the most important yet often overlooked critical differentiator that brings gravitas to a leader's voice: voice quality.

Voice quality, simply put, is how you sound: pitch, volume, pace, rhythm, resonance, etc. All the characteristics of your voice contribute to your overall sound.

1. Pitch: The highness or lowness of the voice, determined by the frequency of vocal cords' vibrations.
2. Volume: The amount or intensity of the sound, often described by most people as the loudness or softness of the voice (though this is not accurate and will be further discussed later in this chapter).
3. Pace: The speed at which words are spoken (fast or slow).
4. Prosody: The rhythm, stress, and intonation patterns in speech, which play a crucial role in conveying emotions, attitudes, and grammatical structure. The voice problem related to prosody is monotone.
5. Resonance: Amplification of the voice through the sound chambers (for example, voice box, chest, etc.) in the body, which can add richness and depth to the sound.

THE VOICE THAT PROJECTS GRAVITAS

Have you heard a tiger roar?

I was blown away the first time I heard a tiger roar. It is so powerful and thunderous that it can travel up to 2 miles (3.2 kilometres)! Yet a tiger's voice is deep. Most people think that a deep voice can't be heard clearly from a distance. The tiger has proven us wrong. Animals from afar run or hide the moment they hear a tiger roar.

The tiger's vocal prowess serves multiple purposes, including communicating its presence to other animals, establishing territory, and intimidating rivals or responding to threats. The tiger's voice is a potent and awe-inspiring aspect of its presence, reflecting its status as one of the most formidable and majestic creatures in the animal kingdom. In China, people call the tiger the "king of the beasts," because the stripes on the tiger's forehead form the Chinese word for "King," "王." King or not, one cannot deny the immense strength, power, formidability, and agility that tigers possess, making them one of nature's most feared and respected predators.

A deep and resonant voice signals strength and power. Animals use vocalisations to communicate their dominant status or to intimidate rivals.

In humans, the perception that a deep and resonant voice is powerful and authoritative can be traced back to the early stages of human evolution. This association has been shaped by biological and historical factors over millions of years.

Going back thousands of years, physical strength and size were crucial for survival. Larger individuals with deeper voices were often perceived as stronger and more dominant. This physical prowess was essential for hunting, defending territory, and protecting the group. As a result, deeper voices became associated with leadership and authority.

From an evolutionary point of view, deeper voices are often linked to higher testosterone levels, which can signal physical strength, power, and influence.

The perception that deep and resonant voices signal power and authority continues to influence human perceptions today. This is true for both men and women [3–5].

MYTHS ON DEEP VOICES

Myth number one

A deep voice is not a low voice. A low voice is one-dimensional, with the pitch going down, and linear. A deep voice is three-dimensional. It has depth and width. It is the result of proper voice projection through relaxation, proper breathing, and full-body resonance, as you'll discover in the next section.

Myth number two

Because a deep and resonant voice conveys gravitas, many people purposely lower their voice pitch.

I asked one client who used this wrong method, "How long did it last?"

"10 to 15 minutes," he replied.

I laughed. "You'll lose all the authority and credibility when your clients see you on the street and realise you sound different."

Purposely lowering your voice is done by pressing your vocal cords down. Over time, you'll damage your vocal cords. Not only that, when you press your vocal cords down, your voice is suppressed, too, rather than being projected out. As a result, people won't hear you clearly. Remember that voice projection is supported by the out breath. When you press your vocal cords down, your breath does not come out. After some time, you'll feel breathless. Because people can't hear you clearly, they may ask you to repeat yourself. This is tiring for everybody.

The "DJ" voice

Karen was a part-time emcee. Because the perception is that an emcee's voice is DJ-like, deep and resonant, she purposely lowered her voice for every event she emceed. She often found herself breathless and exhausted. Her voice would get scratchy after a while. "I'm afraid I've lost the idea about how to speak naturally!" She was frustrated. "I also felt that I had to exert a lot of force while speaking with that low voice."

During our work together, I discovered that she had formed the habit of not using her breath while speaking. That was clearly a habit formed while purposely lowering her voice, which of course contributed to her constant exhaustion and breathlessness. We took some time to train her breath to allow it to exit her body while speaking.

A DJ voice is not a deep voice. Like Karen, many DJs purposely lower their voice by pressing the vocal cords down. However, I cannot reiterate enough the damage this can do, to your vocal cords, your breath, and your body, all of which will take time to correct, repair, and restore.

There is a natural and organic way to develop a deep and resonant voice that'll last for the rest of your life, which you'll learn in the next section.

Myth number three

Some of my Asian female clients and audience members have asked, "Will a deep voice make me sound less feminine?" Though I've coached clients from all over the world and spoken to audiences on five continents, this question is asked mostly in Asia, which makes sense when thinking about the history and cultures in Asia.

In most Asian societies, a relatively high-pitched voice is thought of as gentle and submissive, aligning with the traditional gender roles in which women are the caretakers and in a supportive role to men. This norm has been around for thousands of years and remains in many areas today.

In Japan, women are expected to use honorific language (*keigo*) that is respectful and humble. There are specific speech patterns and vocabulary women use that are considered more feminine. From a young age, Japanese girls are expected to speak in a way that aligns with cultural expectations of being polite, considerate, and non-aggressive. This is particularly important in a culture that values hierarchy and respect for authority.

There is a concept, called *burikko* in Japan or *aegyo* in Korea, that refers to a cute and childlike manner of speaking and behaving. Women, particularly young women, are often expected to speak in this manner to appear more charming and endearing. This includes using a higher-pitched voice, baby talk, and exaggerated facial expressions.

In Vietnam and Thailand, women are expected to be gentle and supportive, and a softer and higher-pitched voice aligns with the traditional gender roles. There are similar cultural norms and expectations in many Asian countries.

Though not all women in these countries universally accept or follow the norms, and women in Asia have been fighting for equality in recent years, the history and cultural influence are still ingrained.

What women in Asia could be concerned with instead is not whether a deep voice makes them sound less feminine but what it means to be feminine, or what femininity is.

Femininity, first of all, has nothing to do with feminism. Every human being has both feminine energy (*yin*) and masculine energy (*yang*), regardless of what gender we identify with.

Feminine energy, or *yin*, includes qualities such as nurturing, emotional, intuitive, non-linear, receptive, relational, surrender, being, flow, fluid, etc., whereas masculine energy (*yang*) includes qualities such as making things happen, doing, mental, results-oriented, goals, linear, logical, protecting, structure, fixed, etc.

If you have more feminine qualities than masculine qualities, you are considered more feminine. Therefore, a deep voice will not make you sound less feminine. It is the qualities inside of you that'll determine whether you are more feminine or masculine.

Louise Hay is a great example of a woman who spoke with a deep and resonant voice yet exuded femininity and grace. She was a pioneer in self-development, a renowned motivational author, and founder of Hay House. We referenced her book, *You Can Heal Your Life*, in Chapter 3. She's also a great example of an embodiment of both femininity and masculinity. Louise Hay is well known for her work on emotional healing and loving oneself; she encouraged people to trust their intuition; her teaching style was nurturing, accepting, and supportive, all of which are associated with femininity. She was also an advocate for taking action and making positive changes. Her personal story of overcoming challenges includes healing after cancer, demonstrating her perseverance and strength, qualities associated with masculinity.

The accomplished actress Michelle Yeoh, in my view, is another example of a woman who speaks with a deep and resonant voice yet exudes femininity and elegance. She has a graceful and elegant demeanour, both on and off screen. In her personal life and through her charitable work, Michelle Yeoh has demonstrated a nurturing and supportive nature, qualities associated with femininity. Michelle Yeoh is also an embodiment of both femininity and masculinity. She is known for performing her own stunts in action films, which showcases her strength and discipline. Michelle Yeoh has taken on challenging roles and broken barriers in the film industry, demonstrating her courage and resilience in the face of adversity. Both examples are qualities related to masculinity.

There are many more female role models – for example, actresses Lucy Liu, Maggie Q, and Natalie Portman – who speak with a deep and resonant voice and embody both femininity and masculinity. A deep and resonant voice does not make you sound less feminine; developing what's inside you – feminine qualities such as nurturing, supportive, relational, and so on – is what matters.

Interestingly and coincidentally, the process of working on your voice trains both your femininity and masculinity. Traits related to femininity include relaxation, nurturing your body to create the environment for your best voice to emerge, letting go of your control, and so forth. Traits related to masculinity include disciplined regular practice to achieve the goal of a powerful voice, persistence, and resilience. As a result, you will acquire a voice with gravitas that's authoritative, considered a more masculine quality. Expressing emotions in your voice (see Chapter 5) is considered a more feminine quality. As you can see, femininity and masculinity are intertwined in the entire process and the results. When you work on your voice, you are working on the balance between your femininity and masculinity. Too much of either will lead to an unbalanced energy, followed by physical dis-ease. What you need is balance.

HOW TO DEVELOP A DEEP AND RESONANT VOICE?

The objective on developing a deep and resonant voice is to develop full resonance; that is, resonance in your whole body. With resonance in your whole body, your voice will deepen as a result, naturally. I call this a "full" voice.

Voice is vibration. The vibration that comes from your breath passing through your vocal cords is very weak and difficult to hear, as a whisper. When you whisper, only your vocal cords vibrate. When you lose your voice or have a sore throat owing to improper projection, stop whispering! This makes the vocal cords work harder and become more inflamed.

We have amplifiers in our bodies that amplify the initial vibration from the vocal cords, allowing us to be heard. The amplifiers are cavities, or sound chambers, including the nose, mouth, throat, voice box, and chest, that amplify the sound through resonance.

To understand how that works, think of a musical instrument such as a guitar, violin, cello, or bass. When you play chords, the initial vibration/sound from the chords activates the box (sound chamber) to resonate, amplifying the sound. You get the idea of how amplification works, even though the musical instrument's chords are not exactly the same as the vocal cords.

Your body is like an orchestra: full-body voice resonance is like having all the musical instruments in your orchestra in play. Most people only use four of the five major instruments: nose, mouth, throat, and voice box. The biggest instrument has not been used or not used to its optimum; that is, your chest.

To develop full resonance in your body, or your full voice, you'll need to activate the chest ("Activation" in Figure 4.1) to participate in

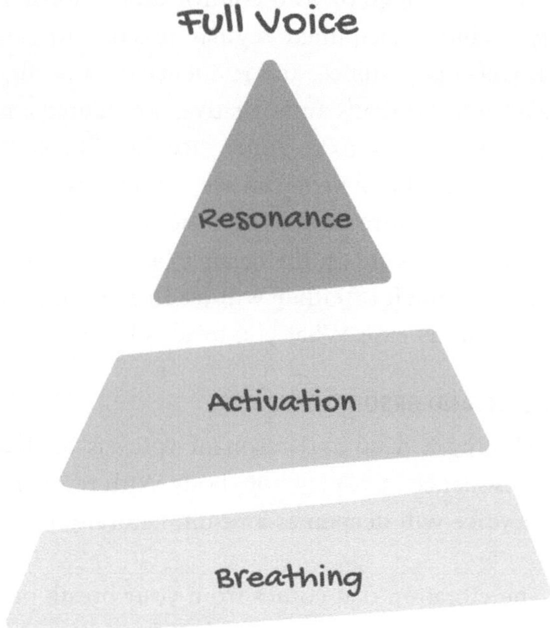

Figure 4.1 Full voice development steps.

the orchestra. Once the chest is activated, together with the other four sound chambers ("Resonance" in Figure 4.1), your voice pitch will naturally deepen, and your voice will project more gravitas, credibility, certainty, authority, and trustworthiness. As a surprising side benefit, because your voice projection now relies on full resonance, you will avoid strains on your vocal cords, and you will never have a sore throat or lose your voice.

To activate the chest cavity as a resonating chamber, you must breathe properly and form a habit of proper diaphragmatic breathing ("Breathing" in Figure 4.1); see the steps on proper breathing in Chapter 3.

WHAT IS RESONANCE?

Resonance is a phenomenon that occurs when a vibrating source or external force (say, "A") drives another system (say, "B") to vibrate at specific frequencies, typically at its natural frequency. This results in a significant increase in the amplitude of the vibration, leading to a more pronounced or intense response.

Imagine there are two tuning forks, A and B. First, you strike A and A starts to vibrate. Here A is the vibrating source or external force. Then, depending on how long it takes for A's vibration to reach B's natural vibrational frequency, A will drive B to vibrate. Now if you were to mute A, you would hear sound coming out of B. The sound or vibration that comes out of B is resonance. If you didn't mute A, the sound would become more intense.

You may have heard someone say, "What you said resonates with me." This is the metaphorical use of "resonance." You said "A" and it evoked the other person's mental or emotional frequency, which is "B." You two are on the same vibrational frequency.

In the voice production process, the vibrating source, "A," is breath passing by the vocal cords. After "A" starts to vibrate, it'll drive "B" to vibrate. "B" includes the nose, mouth, throat, voice box, and chest. Let's call them B1 to B5. The sound generated by "A" is a whisper. Once the Bs start to resonate, your sound – your voice – becomes more audible, stronger, richer, and fuller. Imagine if a guitar had no box (sound chamber) but only six strings – the sound would be unappealing and thin.

For most people, only B1 to B4 are resonating. When you activate B5 (chest), your sound will not only be more resonant but will also have unlimited potential. In an orchestra, when all the instruments are playing at the same time, the sound is more powerful and versatile, able to cover a much wider range.

Let's now have your internal orchestra with various musical instruments polished, activated, and working for you.

DEVELOPING RESONANCE

To develop full resonance, you first need to activate resonance in the chest. The reason most people doe not have chest resonance in their voice production is because they are not breathing properly. As shown in Figure 3.3 in Chapter 3, when you are not breathing properly, your chest cavity is compressed and tense. Even if you want to use it, it's limited and the resonance in the chest is not at its optimum.

Chest resonance, as well as proper breathing, cannot be accessed on demand. They must become second nature, so that even when you are nervous or stressed your voice will be deep and resonant. Each step in Figure 4.1 needs to become a habit.

Activation: Activate your chest to resonate

Remember that tension is the enemy of your voice. When there is tension in the body, the vibration will either stop or be distorted. As a result, your voice won't be in its optimum state.

Before you activate your chest cavity, make sure you are relaxed. You can do some stretches, followed by proper breathing exercises.

Then take a proper breath in where the abdomen moves outward. When you breathe out, gently push your abdomen in, and at the same time, sigh out the breath with the sound "hi" or "ha" until you breathe out all the air in your lungs. The reason we use the word "sound" to describe "hi" or "ha" is that it is a random sighing sound that is not a clear word. If you feel some light vibration in your chest and your vocal cords area feels relaxed, you are doing it correctly. Congratulations! You have just activated your chest cavity.

To enable the chest to resonate at all times, practice the exercise six to eight times a day for 2 to 3 minutes each time, for the next 1½ to 2 months.

Many clients notice after 1 month of practice that in normal daily speaking they feel some sound or vibration in the chest. That's when you'll know you are on the right track.

How do you know if you are doing the exercise correctly?

- Feeling relaxed
  You must feel relaxed before, during, and after the practice. The exercise is basically sighing out with a random sound. The only difference between the exercise and your normal sigh is that the sigh is propelled with proper breath. If your abdomen is tight and tired, you are not doing it correctly.
  The only discomfort you may experience is lightheadedness, similar to what you may experience while doing proper breathing exercises, as a result of hyperventilation. If this happens, pause to rest for a while and breathe slowly. If the symptom persists, this may be due to an underlying health issue and you may wish to consult a healthcare professional.
- Synchronised movement
  The inward movement of your abdomen while breathing out and the sound "hi" or "ha" should be synchronised. The mistake many

clients make is moving the abdomen, followed by a delayed sound from the voice box where the vocal cords use unnecessary effort. In doing so, you are interrupting the natural voice production process.

Clients who made that mistake tried to use their mind to control how the body works, which part should move inward and where it should make sound. Your body is not a puppet. It knows how to function and doesn't need your mind to help it to coordinate.

Clients have asked me, "Am I too stupid to get it right?"

I laugh, "It's the exact opposite. It is because you are too intelligent and trust in the power of your mind. You are trying to use your mind to control how your body should work!"

You need to trust your body. It knows better than you, specifically your mind. All you need to do is relax and breathe out properly as you sigh with a "hi" or "ha" sound. Your body will take care of the rest.

We, as human beings, have more than one intelligence centre that we are most familiar with, the cognitive intelligence centre (for example, being analytical and logical). We also have a body intelligence centre (for example, physical sensations, intuition, etc.) and heart intelligence centre (for example, emotions, human connections).

For voice work, it helps you to develop the two latter intelligence centres. Developing your full voice, including breathing, activation, and resonance, will help you become more attuned to how your body works and senses, thus developing your body intelligence. Speaking with appropriate emotions in your voice (see Chapter 5) focuses on developing your heart intelligence.

Relax your mind. Allow your body to take over during this exercise.

- Unintentional sound

The sound "hi" or "ha" is the result of you breathing out while sighing. You do not need to intentionally use the vocal cords to produce a sound. This is a waste of energy and interrupts how your body naturally functions. The vocal cords know how to work. Relax your mind. Imagine that you are sighing in relief.

- Light sound

The sound "hi" or "ha" is light and weak. It is not loud, nor clear, but airy. If you sense some vibration in the chest, it's good enough. You don't need to put your hand on your chest to see if you sense the vibration. That is not necessarily a sign that you are doing it correctly. Sometimes even when you are doing it incorrectly, you may still sense some vibration in the chest. The key is to check if you are relaxed, breathing properly, and allowing the sound to come out effortlessly.

If the sound of your "hi" or "ha" is loud and clear, it is most likely that you are exerting pressure on the vocal cords, which is incorrect. Instead, observe whether your voice box area is relaxed.

- No movement in your shoulders and chest
  As with proper breathing practice, there should be no movement in your shoulders or chest during this exercise, because when you breathe properly only the abdomen moves in and out with ease.

Measuring your progress

How will your daily voice change with the activation exercise? Do you need to intentionally move your abdomen inward while speaking? These are the questions clients frequently ask. These exercises, including breathing, activation, and resonance, are intended to re-train how your body works. Once your body is re-trained, the change in your voice will happen naturally. You don't need to do anything in your everyday breathing or speaking, but you must take time to practise the exercises.

Many clients are doubtful: "Really? All I have to do is practise daily and my normal voice will change?" Yes – provided that you are practicing the exercises correctly.

Working on your voice is very much like growing a plant. After you plant a seed, you need to create an environment that's conducive for the seed to grow, by watering the seed, loosening the soil, giving it the right amount of sunshine, and so on. The seed does not grow overnight. It takes a few days for growth to appear out of the soil.

When working on your voice, with each step you are creating a conducive environment for your best voice to emerge, by relaxing your body, letting go of your controlling mind, and allowing the breath to sigh out with a sound easily and effortlessly. Your voice won't change immediately: it takes time to re-train your body to remember how it's supposed to work. This requires patience with how your body works.

When clients don't have patience, they purposely lower their voice while speaking in meetings. Or they try intentionally to move the abdomen inward while speaking. These wrong ways of working with your body and voice will confuse your body and interrupt your progress. As a result, you'll have to change another bad habit you have just formed and take even longer to get the voice result you want. If you instead follow the practices regularly, you will progress faster. "Infinite patience brings immediate results" (Wayne Dyer).

Remember, you will start to notice after 1 to 2 months of practice that in your daily normal speaking voice you can feel some sound or vibration in the chest. That's when you'll know you are on the right track and progressing.

Activation is the most challenging step for most clients. It changes how you think voice should work. It is counter-intuitive that the best voice does not come from trying harder or exerting more effort but just the opposite – from being more relaxed. The best voice comes from the most relaxed body. Relaxation is crucial in creating a conducive environment in your body for it to resonate. Many clients realised that when they felt tense, they wouldn't get the practice correctly. Relaxation needs to be observed and practiced throughout the entire full voice development process. If you experience tension in your body, before your practice, go through the exercises Body Scan and Relaxation in Chapter 3.

After you've made progress with chest cavity activation (1 to 2 months), you can move on to develop full resonance.

The good news is that once you are able to practice activation easily and effortlessly, full resonance is easy to develop. Many clients have been surprised: "That's it?! This is easy!" It is easy because you have laid a solid foundation for your body in building a conducive environment from which to generate resonance easily.

Develop full resonance

Relax your body. Place one hand at your belly button area. Breathe in and feel your hand moving outward. On breathing out, activate your chest using the sound "hi" or "ha" and gently push the abdomen inward. Breathe in again. On the next out breath, push your abdomen inward harder on the sound "hi" or "ha." You should feel there is more sound in not only the chest but also in the other four cavities: nose, mouth, throat, and voice box. Meanwhile, your vocal cords' area should be relaxed and no effort should be used during the exercise. That's where you are generating full resonance.

That's all you need to do to generate full resonance; that is, push your abdomen inward harder to produce the sound. It seems so simple that many clients initially doubted: "That's it?" Resonance, simply put, is more sound. How do you get more sound in your body? One, you need to breathe out more to have the vocal cords vibrate more in the first place. Two, have all the five sound chambers/cavities relaxed and ready to use. In the activation exercise, you've activated all the sound chambers, ready for use. All you need to do now is to breathe out more by pushing your abdomen inward harder. Your body will take care of the rest; that is, the sound will come out fully resonant.

Your practice would be to do this exercise six to eight times a day for 2 to 3 minutes each time, provided that proper breathing has become a habit, which takes 1½ to 2 months, and that you have practiced activation exercise for 1½ to 2 months. Thus, you will not practice full resonance exercise for the first 3 to 4 months. Only then will you find full resonance practice to be easy and effortless. Practice full resonance exercises for another 1½ to 2 months. You'll start to notice your daily normal speaking voice getting stronger and deeper, sounding resonant, and projecting gravitas.

Similar to activation exercise, in daily speaking, you don't need to purposely move your abdomen to produce sound. You'll confuse the body and interrupt its process in re-training the body and forming a habit. All you need to do is regular daily practice of full resonance exercise. After 1½ to 2 months, you'll start to notice that your normal speaking voice is changing.

How do you know if you are practicing the exercise correctly? Check points 1, 2, 3, and 5 used for the Activation exercise. That is, you need to feel relaxed before, during, and after practising. You may experience lightheadedness. When that happens, pause to rest for a while and breathe slowly. If the symptom persists, you may wish to consult with a healthcare professional.

Full resonance practice requires you to use more breaths for stronger resonance. This will test whether you have practised proper breathing well and whether you have increased your lung capacity. You can go back to proper breathing practice if you realise you don't have enough breath to sustain resonance while practising.

In full resonance exercise, the inward movement of your abdomen and the full resonance sound should be synchronised. The only difference from activation is that the sound is stronger and more resonant. Avoid using the vocal cords to make intentional sound with effort. Allow the sound to come out more resonant as a result. To make that happen, breathe out more by pushing the abdomen inward harder.

It is a wonderful feeling when you sense your whole body is resonating with sound. You'll realise your body is indeed like a musical instrument, waiting for you to play and discover its rich sound.

VOLUME

Developing full resonance will also solve the issue of a soft voice that cannot project in a large room without shouting. You'll notice that your voice volume is automatically increased and no one will ever ask you to repeat yourself.

> "How come you are loud?"
>
> Yvonne had a soft voice. She often spoke as if she were talking to herself. In meetings, people often asked her to repeat what she had said, which was frustrating for Yvonne as well as her listeners.
>
> As she worked on her voice and progressed with full resonance, she was surprised to share, "We were in the living room talking one night and my son asked, 'Mom, how come you are loud?!'" Yvonne was surprised. "I wasn't shouting at all. It was the resonance! … I was so happy to hear that!"

Resonance intensifies sound. As a result, your volume is naturally increased.

You may have noticed that I use the word "increase" to describe volume, instead of "soft" or "loud." The definition of volume is the amount or intensity of the sound, which is a quantitative degree of change. There's no pitch change involved, which is the high and low of your voice. For "loud," the pitch goes up, so it's not really a volume change. For amount, intensity, or quantity, using the word soft or loud to describe is not accurate, nor is turning the volume up or down, though that's what almost everyone uses. Increasing or decreasing the volume might be more accurate of a description for a quantity or intensity change, and the word small or big might also be more accurate, even though it may sound weird. Alternatively, we can use the word quiet or strong to describe volume. Those are the words you'll see in the book.

To speak with gravitas, you should avoid speaking with a "loud" voice, which can come across as aggressive, shallow, and emotionally unstable, let alone unpleasant to the ears. Instead, speak with a stronger voice with full resonance. You'll convey more seriousness, credibility, and certainty.

Some clients have asked, "Will a stronger or deeper voice sound unclear?" The answer is no. Think about the tiger we talked about earlier. A tiger has a deep voice that resonates up to 3.2 kilometres. It's not that a deep voice is unclear but that you haven't learned how to use the right volume level to project clearly, to not only be heard but also to convey gravitas.

Resonance is the key to changing your volume levels. To speak at different volume levels, all you need to change is the amount of the breath you use. For a quiet voice, you'll use less breath and for a stronger voice, you'll use more breath, provided you have formed habits of speaking with a full voice (see Figure 4.1).

THE POWER OF FULL VOICE RESONANCE

"You become happier"

Vernon looked depressed when he first came to me. He wanted to develop a more powerful voice so he would be more visible in cross-function meetings and presentations. He was experiencing job insecurity due to the poor economic environment coupled with layoffs in the company. This insecurity was impacting him outside of work as well. I seldom saw him smile; instead, he looked anxious all the time, as if there was something very heavy dragging him down and chaining him to the ground.

As he progressed towards a resonant voice, I slowly saw the heaviness easing. He looked lighter in both complexion and mood. He looked agile and moved with flow and ease. In one session, he shared, "I presented to the CEO today and it went so well that the CEO said, 'You'll be the one doing all the future presentations!'"

"Goodbye job insecurity!" I congratulated him. "You are the most valuable asset now!"

When we concluded the final session, Vernon asked, "Cynthia, what is the biggest change you saw in me?"

"You became happier," I responded in an instant.

"I think so, too," he agreed. "Now I am more patient with my daughter, and she is happier, too."

How interesting and true. When one person becomes happier, the ripple effect is tremendous.

When I shared this story with a friend, he commented, "You are changing people's lives." It dawned on me at that moment that my friend was right. That gave me more affirmation that I am on the right path in fulfilling my life's purpose. It was not only Vernon but many clients who became happier through our work together. As they developed full resonance in their voices, their appearances changed, too. They glowed and looked powerful. Indeed, many clients have commented, "It's like magic!"

Voice is vibration. Everyone's unique voice sends out a specific vibrational frequency. Your current voice sends out the frequency that reflects the current state of you, including physical, mental, emotional, and even spiritual. Your current state might be distorted due to physical tension, stuck emotions, accumulated trauma, negative experiences, etc. And your voice reflects all of that. Working on your voice, or your vibrational frequency, changes your current state. Full resonance, full and optimised vibration, changes – in fact, optimises and uplifts – your vibrational frequency. Many clients have shared, "I don't know why, but I just feel good."

Mind and body are one. When you change your mind – for example, to feel more confident mentally – you'll look and sound more confident. On the other hand, when you work on your body – for example, with yoga practice – you'll feel more peaceful; if you stand in a power pose [6], you'll feel more powerful; if you speak with a fully resonant voice, you'll feel more elevated. What's even better is that people around you will unconsciously respond positively to this elevated you.

Career advanced by two levels

Melissa was rejected twice for promotion by her boss. "You don't sound as powerful as the next level requires," she told her. She felt despair and was stuck, not being able to see career advancement in her current company. To make it worse, she wasn't having much luck in her search for a new job either. She decided to work on her voice.

As she progressed to full resonance, she was surprised to notice that people became more attentive when she spoke and showed her respect more than she had expected, even in social settings. She once briefly shared in a women's social network and people responded, "What you said was so powerful." Melissa said, "I can't believe it. It was just a random sharing!"

Before our final session, she was very happy to report that she received a promotion that advanced her position by two levels. "Now when I talk, I can see the impact I have on people."

Clients who have developed full resonance in their voices noticed that other people are more attentive and respectful, and their influence has increased.

We met Briana in Chapter 2, who observed that her staff started following her instructions without any doubts or arguments. It was not because she was fierce – just the opposite. She was seen as a very understanding leader but now when she spoke, her voice carried influence and authority.

No wonder many clients have shared, "Whatever Morgan Freeman sells, I'll just buy." He is known for a deep and resonant voice that conveys trustworthiness, credibility, and authority. Former British Prime Minister Margaret Thatcher dropped her voice almost half an octave to convey authority and command respect. For leaders who want to speak with gravitas, project a commanding presence, and unite people with their influence, full resonance is a covert advantage.

PAUSE

Many clients have shared, "I love how Barack Obama used pauses in his speeches." Pause is a powerful tool in speaking with gravitas.

"I should pause more often." Almost all of my clients have said that after watching their own recorded speeches. Most people realise the importance of pause, but few are able to do it well.

"I have too much content to cover. I don't have time to pause." Cut your content and focus more on delivering with impact. Both Barack Obama and Bill Clinton averaged 100 words per minute during their speeches, 30% slower than a typical conversational rate of 150 words, largely due to their strategic pauses.

Neuroscience provides compelling evidence for the benefits of pausing [7]. When we pause, we engage the prefrontal cortex, the part of the brain responsible for executive functions such as logical thinking, decision making, and emotion regulation. This engagement helps your listeners to absorb what you've presented and process the information more thoroughly, making your message more impactful.

Pausing also activates the parasympathetic nervous system, which helps to calm the body and mind [8]. This physiological response reduces stress and anxiety, allowing you as a speaker to stay centred and composed. As a leader who wants to speak with gravitas and impact, you cannot ignore the power of pause.

Where and when to pause?

After speaking to a group of professional speakers, one person approached me and said, "I love the way you used pauses." I had never thought about where and when to use pauses. Imagine you are listening to a speaker where all of the pauses are so deliberately crafted. How will that make you feel as an audience member? When you focus too much on where and when to use pauses, you'll lose focus on your audience. An unengaged audience is an unmoved audience.

There are rules of thumb for using pauses. The golden rule is to ask yourself often, "What do I want the people to do or feel with what I've just said?" How you want what you say to influence the audience comes first, not the other way around.

- Pause for presence

  Before you utter your first word in front of a group, look around at the audience to establish your presence. This shows your confidence and composure and is where you build connection with people. If you are nervous, you can calm yourself down by taking a few proper deep breaths.

  Many speakers just walk onto the stage and start speaking without letting people see them first. This can come across as rushed and lacking confidence. People need to see and acknowledge the person speaking to them.
- Pause for suspense

  Curiosity is a cornerstone in keeping people engaged. To keep people's attention, you'll need to build suspense to keep them wondering, "What happens next?" Think about your favourite movies or TV drama series – it's the suspense that keeps you hooked to watch until the end.

  This is where the way you structure what you say is as important as the way you deliver it. To pause for suspense, there first needs to be suspense! Many clients have come to me and said, "I've already got the speech and just need to work on my voice delivery to keep them engaged." When I looked at the speech – "Good morning, everyone! Today I'll share with you the latest project updates" – I sighed. "No matter how engaging your voice is, 'Good morning' is not going to get them hooked."

  Instead, think about how you can say it in a way that makes people think, "Yes, tell me more!" It could be something along the lines as, "Today, you'll hear three major updates that'll save half your effort."

There are two major differences in the restructured line. One, it uses the word "you." Two, it talks about how it'll benefit the listeners: "save half your effort." Your audience needs to know, "What's in it for me?" This is one example.

Once you have the suspense, you can deliver with curiosity. For example, record yourself speaking the sentence in the example above, "Today, you'll hear three major updates that'll save half your effort" and then listen to it to see whether you will pique people's attention and make them say, "Yes, tell me more!"

If you want your audience to feel curious about what you'll say, you'll pause, preferably automatically, to pique their curiosity, thereby keeping their attention, too. That means you'll pause after the word "save" and then continue with "half your effort." Avoid adding more words after that, which will weaken the effect and impact of the "punch line"; that is, "half your effort."

Many clients tend to add more words, especially if they feel they are failing to deliver curiosity. Don't add more words. Instead, practice pausing for suspense more effectively.

How long should you pause? A greater concern would be, did you pique their curiosity? A pause may be 2 to 3 seconds, but when you are speaking, you don't want to count this out to yourself. You'll lose your connection with the audience. Instead, observe your listeners – you'll know when you can deliver the punch line.

In standup comedy, a punch line is the line that makes people laugh. The setup is followed by the punch line. Before you deliver the punch line, you pause to build anticipation and to get a bigger laugh when you deliver the punch line. For example, comedian Chris Rock's famous line, "There are only three things women need in life: food, water, and compliments." The setup is the line before "compliments." You'll pause after the word "and" and then deliver the punch line, or punch word in this case: "compliments."

Comedian Jerry Seinfeld famously joked, "According to most studies, people's number one fear is public speaking. Number two is death. Death is number two. Does that sound right? This means to the average person, if you go to a funeral, you're better off in the casket than doing the eulogy."

The punch line is "in the casket." My personal opinion is to move that to the end and restructure the sentence, if you are not as famous as Seinfeld. Remember to say nothing after the punch line. If you were to deliver this original line, here's how you can do it for maximum impact and effect: before "in the casket," pause, deliver the line, then pause again to wait for the laughter to fade, followed by "doing the eulogy" for a secondary laugh.

If you ever use humour in your speeches, make sure you pause before you deliver the punch line. Yes, even when you need to speak with gravitas, you often need humour to provide levity. We'll talk about that later in this chapter.

- Pause for reflection

This is the most powerful yet least used pause. Most people are aware that they need to pause for people to digest and reflect on what they've said but don't do so. Many are not comfortable with silence. However, when you are speaking, it's not about you but about how much your audience is able to understand and digest.

You pause not because you want to take a break from speaking. You pause because you want what you say to have an impact. People are only influenced when they have time to reflect on how what they've heard applies to their own lives.

Pausing to give people time to reflect doesn't require planning ahead. That can distract you from what you want to deliver. And it won't help if you're asked to speak on the spot! The key is to shift your focus to the audience, constantly observing how they are receiving your message and whether you need to have them reflect on what you've just said and how much time you need to give them for reflection.

When pausing for reflection, your voice needs to use a downward inflection, also known as a down tone, not an upward inflection, or up tone, as if everything were a question. A downward inflection indicates a statement. Even if you are asking a question, you will use a downward inflection and then pause to allow people time to reflect.

One occasion deserves to be highlighted when it comes to pause for reflection: that is, when you ask a rhetorical question, an answer is not expected. For example, "What will happen if you continue with the same old behaviour?" Make sure when you deliver this rhetorical question you are using a downward inflection; then pause to invite people to reflect without verbally answering the question.

On a side note, if you want to convince, persuade, or influence people to take action, use rhetorical questions rather than spelling out the benefits or consequences. It sounds less demanding and encourages people to reflect on their own lives and make decisions for themselves. This is where the power of the pause for reflection lies.

- Pause for lasting impact

  This is also a type of pausing for reflection. It can be so powerful and worth singling it out. This should be used after you've finished your last words of a speech – and hopefully your last words are not "thank you."

  When a pianist finishes playing the last note, they don't immediately turn to the audience to thank them. They pause to allow the piece of the music to linger in people's minds and hearts, before bowing to the audience.

  Similarly, when you finish saying your profound last words, pause to allow them to linger and have a lasting impact. Craft your last words carefully. Don't rush to the end and dismiss people with a "thank you." Even though your words are finished, your impact is not. Take your time and make what you say count.

- Functional pauses

  When the crowd gets noisy, pause is the best way to get people quiet down and return their attention to you.

  Avoid using filler words: "um," "you know," "I mean," and so on. Notice your tendency to use them and pause to replace them. People often use filler words when they are trying to find the next words or organise their thoughts. Instead, learn how to think on your feet.

  When you are asked a question, listen attentively, and pause before you answer. This gives you time to gather your thoughts and demonstrates your respect and appreciation of the person.

  Great leaders are masters of pauses, because they know,

> "Silence at the right moment is more expressive and commanding than words."
>
> – Cicero

PACE

Leaders who speak with gravitas take their time to speak. As mentioned in the section on pause, both Barack Obama and Bill Clinton averaged 100 words per minute in their speeches, 30% slower than a typical conversational rate of 150 words.

It's not only in speeches or presentations that you need to speak slowly but also in everyday conversation. Speaking slowly conveys your confidence and authority. It adds weight and gravitas to what is being said.

People who speak slowly are seen as knowledgeable and wise. Wisdom is often linked with patience. Speaking slowly can be seen as a sign of patience because you take your time to ensure that your message is understood, rather than rushing through it.

A slower pace can make your speech more influential by giving people time to absorb and process what you've said and feel the impact of your words.

Speaking fast doesn't make you appear as competent or confident – contrary to what many of my clients thought. People who speak fast are often seen as nervous, impatient, and inconsiderate. Speaking fast indicates a desire to finish what you want to say, without considering how well people are receiving the messages. It can also convey a desire to impress people with your knowledge, which can come across as egotistic.

However, you need to strike a balance. Speak too slowly and your audience will become restless, bored and detached from your message.

The recommended speaking rate is 120 to 150 words per minute, but this is not always practical to apply. There are other factors to take into account in addition to your speaking rate. For example, is English your first language? What's your audience's first language? How complex is your topic? Instead, observe the reaction from your listeners and see how well they are absorbing and digesting what you are saying. If you are often asked to slow down, you are obviously going too fast.

How do you slow down? The good news, and perhaps surprising, is that many clients have found after they developed full resonance their speaking rate slowed down automatically. One client compared two recorded live speeches, one from before and one from after our coaching sessions, and was surprised to notice that he spoke more slowly without the need to remind himself to slow down. Another solution is speaking with emotion, which we'll discuss in the next chapter. Many clients have found that their speaking rate slows down automatically when they speak with emotion.

Though speaking slowly is usually better than speaking fast, some situations require faster speech; for example, when you want to build momentum. Take a look at the following excerpt from a speech given by Winston Churchill.

"I can answer in one word, victory, victory at all costs, victory in spite of all terror, victor, however long and hard the road may be. For without victory, there is no survival."

The three sentences on victory escalate the emotion of determination. To have a stronger impact and demonstrate your determination as a leader that nothing is going to stop you from leading your country to victory, your pace would increasingly quicken on these three sentences.

The mistake most clients made was speaking so quickly that nothing they said lingered in people's minds, as if a strong wind passed by and took everything away. In the example above, as your pace quickens, slow down on the underlined words with emphasis, so you can make an impact that lingers in people's minds.

Another occasion in which building momentum is needed is when describing a chaotic situation, to stir people's minds and wake them up to taking action. For example, one client was to deliver the following:

> The world is grappling with a multitude of challenges that contribute to a sense of chaos and uncertainty. Geopolitical tensions continue to escalate in various regions; climate change remains a pressing issue with extreme weather events and natural disasters; economic instability, exacerbated by inflation and supply chain disruptions.

A faster pace will help escalate the seriousness of the issue and create a sense of urgency to act.

Later in the speech, if you want people to feel "hopeful," your pace will slow down. When you are speaking, your pace varies not with advanced planning but is based on how you want people to feel.

CERTAINTY

When leaders speak with certainty, their communication is more compelling and evokes trust. During times of uncertainty and crisis, leaders who can provide a sense of stability and direction are invaluable. They help people to mitigate fear and anxiety, providing a beacon of hope and a clear path forward.

A voice that conveys certainty is grounded. When you've developed gravitas in your voice – that is, a voice with full resonance – you will exude certainty when you speak.

"I sound like I'm crying all the time."

Stephanie led a regional team and reluctantly watched a short clip of a video of herself speaking at a regional meeting. "I sound like I'm crying all the time, even when I'm not nervous!" This didn't project confidence or evoke trust from her team or her boss. "Is there any hope to change it at all?" she asked during our first session.

"When your voice is trembling even when you are not nervous, you are relying too much on your vocal cords, voice box, and throat to project your voice," I replied. "We'll help you learn how to let your body participate so your voice can sound stable. That is the voice I call a 'full' voice. One key step is, of course, working on your breathing."

"Ah, yes!," she said and shared, "I often feel breathless when speaking, too."

As Stephanie progressed, she noticed that she sounded much more stable when viewing recordings of herself speaking.

A voice that conveys certainty is stable. Stability comes from full-body resonance, which has the effect of stabilising your voice. When full resonance becomes a habit, even when you are nervous, your voice will always sound stable, with no trembling or shivering. If your voice trembles on a regular basis even when you are not nervous, as Stephanie's did, learning to speak with full voice will help.

"I sound like an insecure young girl."

Lena was a thought leader and wanted to project more authority when she spoke. She noticed when watching her marketing videos, "I sound like an insecure young girl."

Talking with Lena, I noticed she had another habit: she dragged words out, which made her sound insecure. "Are you a people pleaser?" I asked.

"I am. I have been working on that," she replied. Then she asked, "Does that show in the voice?"

"Voice shows everything about us," I answered.

A voice that conveys certainty sounds mature and secure. Maturity can be developed with a full voice. Insecurity can show up in the voice through different ways. In Lena's case, it showed in her tendency to drag words out in an attempt to appear approachable and friendly. Unfortunately, that also came across as people pleasing and insecure. For example, when she said, "In this video," she elongated the syllable "de" so that it sounded like, "In this videeeeeo." This is not to say that a voice of certainty can't be approachable or friendly; rather, it is meant to have you pay attention to not dragging words out too frequently or when it's not necessary. Your words need to be crisp.

A voice that conveys certainty is firm. If you end your sentences in an upward inflection, that makes you sound like you are asking a question, as if you are not sure what you are talking about. If it's a statement, use a downward inflection. If your voice fades at the end of a sentence, it sounds as if you don't have enough breath – which could be the case if proper breathing is not a habit. Make sure you don't use all your breath to finish one sentence. Instead, emphasise words as you speak, after which you should inhale automatically so you have another breath to sustain the rest of your sentence.

As a leader, your job is not to please people but to inspire and empower them to achieve collective goals and drive your organisation forward. This requires you to sound firm and certain, especially when making tough decisions and handling crises. People follow leaders they can trust and have confidence in, not simply those who are nice.

GRAVITY VERSUS LEVITY

Some clients have asked me, "Will a voice with gravitas make me sound too serious or unapproachable?"

Let's discuss the different roles that gravity and levity play and how to balance them.

Gravity, or gravitas in your voice, is necessary when addressing critical issues with an appropriate level of seriousness. As a leader, you must make tough decisions that can have significant consequences for your team and organisation. This requires a deep understanding of the situation, careful consideration of all factors, and a willingness to take responsibility for the outcomes.

Levity is the opposite of gravity in terms of mood and tone. It's the quality of being lighthearted or humorous. Levity is used to diffuse tension, make challenging situations more bearable, and make difficult conversations less difficult. Levity is achieved by expressing lighter emotions, covered in the next chapter, and speaking with humour.

Gravity ensures that important matters are addressed with the necessary seriousness, and levity can bring a sense of relief, maintain morale, and foster creativity. Great leaders balance the two opposing forces. The balance is not about switching between extremes but rather about integrating both aspects seamlessly into your leadership speaking style.

Lee Kuan Yew, the founding father of Singapore, was known for his serious and pragmatic approach to governance. He could address complex and critical issues with gravity, providing clear and decisive leadership. However, he also had a lighter side, occasionally using humour and anecdotes to connect with his audience and make his points more relatable.

Winston Churchill, known for his powerful and inspiring speeches during World War II, could address the gravity of the situation with eloquence and seriousness. He also had a knack for wit and humour, often using lighthearted remarks to connect with his audience and alleviate tension.

Richard Branson, the founder of the Virgin Group, is known for his adventurous spirit and innovative approach to business. He can discuss serious business matters with gravity but also has a playful and humourous side, often using levity to engage with his audience and inspire creativity and innovation.

"Do Schools Kill Creativity?"

Sir Ken Robinson's TED Talk, "Do Schools Kill Creativity?" [9], is a master class in balancing gravity and levity to deliver a powerful and engaging message.

He addresses a serious and weighty topic, the impact of the current education system on creativity. He argues that schools are designed around the needs of industrialism and are not adequately fostering creativity and innovation. To emphasise the gravity of the situation, Robinson uses data and evidence to support his claims. He conveys a sense of urgency, emphasising the need for immediate action and reform.

He also uses humour throughout his talk to engage the audience and make his points more memorable. For example, he jokes about the similarities between Death Valley and the public education system or the idea of professors as disembodied heads. He also shares lighthearted anecdotes, such as the story of a little girl drawing a picture of God or the tale of Matt Groening creating *The Simpsons*. These anecdotes not only illustrate his points but also provide moments of levity.

Robinson seamlessly balances gravity and levity throughout his talk. That makes his talk not only informative and thought-provoking but also enjoyable and memorable.

> **Inspire people in times of uncertainty**
>
> The following is an example from a client who was preparing to deliver a speech. Try the process yourself and see how you might craft and deliver the speech.
>
> First, describe the uncertainty or chaotic situations faced by your organisation or team using your voice of gravitas to convey the seriousness of the situation to make people realise the seriousness of these issues.
>
> Then reassure people using levity to alleviate the tension and anxiety using a reassuring voice.
>
> End by emphasizing the urgency to act, using a voice full of gravitas.

Following is an example of this type of speech, for reference.

In the time of crisis, most people are lost, confused, and panicking. They look for people who can give them certainty, assurance, and hope. [This paragraph emphasises the gravity of the issue.]

If you are one of them, stop looking around. No, it's not your neighbour sitting beside you. Look at him. He might be even more panicked than you are! [Here humour is used to lighten things up and ease the tension. Tone is critical, or it'll come across as offensive.]

It's time for YOU to wake up, show up, and serve up. It is uncertain times like these that test your resilience. [This paragraph reiterates the gravity and calls for responsibility and action.]

The truth is that everyone initially feels confused and panicky. It is part of being human. When we are faced with something unfamiliar and something dangerously new, our first reaction is the fight-or-flight response. What matters is what happens after your initial reaction. Are you going to continue feeling panic and thus behave irrationally, or are you going to take a step back and re-evaluate the situation? [This paragraph connects with people through empathy and reassures them that it is okay to feel what they are feeling, using levity. It then calls for action with a rhetorical question delivered with gravitas.]

HUMOUR

Humour doesn't mean cracking jokes. It comes with observation of life, people, and their behaviours; quick wit; and practice.

You may know me as a voice coach. You may not know that the two comments I receive the most from my audiences around the world are, "Your session is very engaging" and "Your session is so entertaining."

You don't have to be a standup comedian. Here are some quick and simple humour techniques to help you add levity in your speaking.

The key to using humour is in its unexpectedness. As mentioned earlier in the section on pause, in standup comedy there are setups and punch lines. The setup is where you lead people in one direction, and the punchline is the unexpected derail.

For example, "To get out of a breakup, I've started reading to improve myself. In the books I've read, I learned to release my anger, love myself, and find the strongest words to condemn the ex-boyfriend."

"... to condemn the ex-boyfriend" is the punchline; before that, it's all setup.

Humour is also about self-deprecation. You are showing people that you are not better than them. It shows that you are still a work in progress, like not being able to forgive yet, in the example above. And, yes, that was a line from a speech I gave.

Here's an example where an audience member provided some levity. I asked, "Have you thought about where your voice is from?"

One audience member shouted, "From God!"

"From God" is the punch line. As an unexpected answer, it made the audience laugh.

"These challenges pushed me to the lowest point in my entire life. I couldn't sleep for days. I couldn't see an end. I was hopeless. In those darkest nights, I looked at my bank account and thought, 'Which bank should I rob?'"

The humour in this example helps release the tension built up before the punch line. Many speakers keep building the tension and the audience begins to feel uncomfortable or even awkward, not knowing what they should do or whether they should say anything. It's like a rubber band: when you keep on building the tension by stretching it more and more, it breaks. One mistake many speakers make is that, instead of using humour, they lead the audience to the lowest point, making them miserable, and then say, "But all that's in the past now." The audience will feel cheated. Humour is a delicate job. You are working with people's emotions, so make sure you take care of them.

When it comes to using your voice for delivery, the use of a pause before the punch line cannot be emphasised enough. The inflection before and while delivering the punch line should be in opposite tones.

For example, before "to condemn the ex-boyfriend," the voice sounds serious because the speaker sounds very serious about improving herself; on the punch line, the pitch is higher to show the unresolved anger.

For the example on the "bank robbery," before the punchline, "Which bank should I rob?" the voice sounds more and more depressed, and on the punchline, the voice becomes lighthearted.

The real secret to humour that I've found over the years is living a joyful life. Being joyful doesn't mean you are happy all the time. Sadness, anger, grief, etc., are all necessary and natural human emotions. There are three principles I use to help lead a joyful life.

- Nothing is really a big deal.
  When you grasp something too tightly, you know what will happen. It might break. You never feel relaxed and everyone around you is all worked up. Good luck having a creative and productive working environment.
- Don't take everything too seriously.
  Lighten up. Laugh at yourself. If you can't, laugh at others – just don't tell them!
- Don't worry.
  Worry is torturing yourself with something that hasn't happened. Not worrying does not mean you don't care about the future or the possible consequences. It means doing your best and leaving the rest to God, or a higher power, or whatever you believe in.

May you live a joyful life that's full of laughter!

REFERENCES

[1] Wikipedia. (2024). "Gravitas." https://en.wikipedia.org/wiki/Gravitas

[2] Cicero, M.T. (1942). *De Oratore*. Trans. E. W. Sutton and H. Rackham. Cambridge: Loeb Classical Library, Harvard University Press.

[3] Mayew, W. J., Parsons, C. A., and Venkatachalam, M. (2013). "Voice Pitch and the Labor Market Success of Male Chief Executive Officers." *Evolution & Human Behavior*, 34(4), 243–248.

[4] Anderson, R. C., and Klofstad, C. A. (2012). "Preference for Leaders with Masculine Voices Holds in the Case of Feminine Leadership Roles." *PLoS ONE*, 7(12), e51216. doi:10.1371/journal.pone.0051216

[5] Tigue, C. C., Borak, D. J., O'Connor, J. J., Schandl, C. A., and Feinberg, D. R. (2012). "Voice Pitch Influences Voting Behavior." *Evolution and Human Behavior*, 33(3), 210–216.

[6] Cuddy, A. (2012). "TEDGlobal." https://www.ted.com/talks/amy_cuddy_your_body_language_may_shape_who_you_are?subtitle=en

[7] Arnsten, A. F. T. (2009). "Stress Signaling Pathways That Impair Prefrontal Cortex Structure and Function." *Nature Reviews Neuroscience*, 10(6), 410–422.

[8] Porges, S. W. (2007). "The Polyvagal Perspective." *Biological Psychology*, 74(2), 116–143.

[9] Robinson, K. (2006). "TED2006." https://www.ted.com/talks/sir_ken_robinson_do_schools_kill_creativity?subtitle=en

Five

"Great leaders move us. They ignite our passion and inspire the best in us. When we try to explain why they are so effective, we speak of strategy, vision, or powerful ideas. But the reality is much more primal: Great leadership works through the emotions."

– *Daniel Goleman*, Primal Leadership: Unleashing the Power of Emotional Intelligence

THE DOMINANCE AND SUPERIORITY OF LOGIC

"Oh, no, no, no. I can't show my emotions at work." Many clients have been resistant to the idea of speaking with emotion.

Logical left brain thinking is dominant in today's business world. This mode of thinking, characterised by analytical reasoning, problem-solving, and linear thought processes, has revolutionised society's progress in many ways; for example, algorithms, artificial intelligence, and machine learning have transformed industries and made breakthroughs in medical research, financial modelling, and consumer behaviour analysis. Logical left brain thinking has also helped business leaders in data-driven decision-making, strategic planning, and performance metrics.

This logical way of thinking has undoubtedly driven significant progress and thus is often thought as superior. However, over-reliance on this mode has unintended consequences; for example, a lack of empathy can result in ineffective communication, unmotivated or even resentful team members, and a higher employee turnover rate; focusing too much on logic can make leaders appear factual, insensitive, and boring, which can fail to engage and inspire people; the prioritisation of logic can lead leaders to struggle with building trusting relationship with their team members, peers, and stakeholders; and a lack of emotional connection can make it difficult to foster a sense of belonging among team members, resulting in a dearth of loyalty and support.

DOI: 10.4324/9781003596486-5

THE POWER OF EMOTIONS IN LEADERSHIP SPEAKING

If you want to engage and connect with people, you need to speak with emotion. If you want to motivate and inspire people, you can't do it without emotional expression. If you want to convince and persuade people, you can't do it by logic alone. Logic makes people think; emotion makes people act.

Martin Luther King Jr., the civil rights leader, was renowned for his powerful and emotionally charged speeches, most notably his "I Have a Dream" address. His words resonated with the struggles and aspirations of millions, inspiring a movement for social justice.

Pope Francis, the leader of the Catholic Church, was famous for his emotionally resonant messages of love, compassion, and social justice. His speeches and writings often addressed the emotional and spiritual needs of people around the world.

Malala Yousafzai, the young Pakistani activist and Nobel Peace Prize laureate, is known for her emotionally powerful speeches advocating for girls' education and human rights. Her personal story and passionate advocacy have inspired people globally.

At the core of your leadership communication is the ability to influence people. Emotions are powerful drivers of human behaviour and decision-making. When you express emotions authentically, you tap into the emotions of your audience, making your message more compelling and memorable.

Emotional expression builds trust and credibility. Authentic leaders who openly express their emotions are often perceived as more genuine and trustworthy. This authenticity fosters a deeper connection with your followers, encouraging open communication and collaboration. When you are honest about your feelings, you create an environment where others feel safe in expressing their emotions as well, leading to more transparent and productive conversations.

Emotions are contagious. *Emotional contagion* is a phenomenon in which the emotions expressed by a leader can ripple through an organisation, influencing the overall mood and culture. Positive emotions, such as optimism and enthusiasm, can foster a supportive and productive work environment. Conversely, negative emotions like stress and pessimism can hinder creativity and collaboration. Effective leaders are mindful of their emotional impact and strive to cultivate a positive emotional climate.

Expressing one's emotions does not mean "being emotional." As a leader, you must be self-aware, with an understanding your emotions and their impact on others. You must also be skilled in self-regulation, managing your emotions in a way that supports your leadership goals. Without emotional intelligence, you may struggle to communicate emotions effectively, leading to misunderstandings, conflict, or disengagement.

EMOTIONS AND LEADERSHIP PRESENCE

In Chapter 4 we talked about leadership presence as a leader's ability to create connection and inspire others. It is how you make people feel when you are with them.

Emotional expression play a crucial role in enhancing your leadership presence. When you express authentic emotions while speaking, you come across as genuine, relatable, and approachable, and you are able to build a deeper connection with people. This fosters trust and is essential to the support you need for your organisation.

People are inspired and motivated when you tap into their emotions. Emotionally charged messages are more memorable and impactful. Imagine how different the outcome would have been if Martin Luther King Jr. had delivered an emotionless speech. There might have been no movement for social justice! Or if Winston Churchill had said, "Never give in, never, never, never, never" with no feeling. The British would not have placed their trust and faith in him and would not have fought as hard. Imagine Mother Teresa saying, "Spread love everywhere you go. Let no one ever come to you without leaving happier" without expressing compassion – her legacy, one of service to humanity – would not have been of such magnitude.

No emotion conveys a type of emotion

Eileen holds a monthly team sales meeting. At a monthly sales review, she said, "Alright, last month John and Jane did well, exceeding the target by 20%; Aaron and Alex didn't meet the target and need to catch up."

Although she thought she sounded objective, unfortunately, instead she came across as cold and demanding. John said, "Your tone made us feel like exceeding 20% is no big deal, that we should have achieved more than that!" Clearly, that wasn't Eileen's intention.

"You may have thought you didn't express any emotion. But no emotion conveys a type of emotion," I told her. "Your team perceived you as cold and demanding. Be sure you know what emotion you want people to feel before you speak so you can convey exactly that."

> **Masculine presence versus feminine presence**
>
> Carmen was competing to be a senior VP in her company. "I have no problem asserting myself and conveying authority, perhaps sometimes even intimidating to my staff. But that's what got me here. However, the company is now promoting female leaders who are warmer and friendlier. I need help with that."
>
> "We can't just simply teach you how to sound warm and friendly. There are techniques, but you'll need to feel it, from the inside out. If not, you'll come across as inauthentic," I said. "You need to learn how to feel and express empathy and caring."

This is a dilemma faced by many female clients, relying on their masculine traits to get ahead at work. Somehow along the way, they lose their feminine presence. As we discussed in the last chapter, femininity is not having a girly or sweet voice but is evident in qualities such as nurturing, intuitive, non-linear, receptive, relational, etc., as well as the ability to express emotions, especially empathy and compassion. Continue to use the masculine qualities such as making things happen, being results-oriented, and so on, while developing your feminine qualities. Great female leaders and successful women achieve a balance between masculinity and femininity. In addition to Louise Hay, Michelle Yeoh, and Lucy Liu, Aung San Suu Kyi and Queen Elizabeth II are another two great examples.

Gender stereotypes may play a role in inhibiting emotional expression among male leaders. The expression of emotions, such as empathy or vulnerability, is often seen as feminine. If you are a male leader, you may feel pressured to conform to traditional masculine norms. Speaking with emotion, however, is not the same as "being emotional"; instead, it means expressing appropriate emotions. Great leaders, such as Martin Luther King Jr., Winston Churchill, and Lee Kuan Yew, speak with the balance between logics and emotions, masculinity and femininity.

AUTHENTICITY AND EMOTIONAL EXPRESSIONS

Authenticity is the alignment between a leader's internal values and beliefs and their external behaviours and actions.

Authentic leaders are open and honest in their communications. This transparency builds trust and fosters engagement and commitment among their team. When leaders are true to themselves, they make their team members feel safe in expressing their authentic thoughts, feelings, and ideas, resulting in a more motivated and better performing team.

"Being professional means that you can't show your emotions at work."

May was one of the top candidates for a senior leadership role in her company. Her staff has always viewed her as a working machine, distant and with no emotions, which also was reflected in her voice. "I think that's my professionalism," May shared. "Being professional means that you can't show your emotions at work. That's what got me where I am."

During our work together, I got to know her better and encouraged her to share her personal stories with the staff. At a company event, some people were talking about kids with autism. She approached the group and shared how she dealt with the challenges of raising a child with autism. Afterwards, a few people came up to her and said, "Thank you for sharing. It was very inspiring." May was surprised and told me, "My vulnerability inspired people." At work, she noticed that people were starting to open up to her.

Emotional expression is a powerful tool to enhance your authenticity as a leader. When you openly express your emotions, you demonstrate your humanness and vulnerability, making you more relatable and approachable.

One of the key ways emotional expression enhances authenticity is by promoting self-awareness. When you are in touch with your emotions, you are better equipped to understand your own motivations, strengths, and weaknesses. This self-awareness enables you to communicate more genuinely and effectively, aligning your words and actions with your true self. By acknowledging and expressing your emotions, you can also gain valuable insights into your values, priorities, and passions, helping you to make more authentic decisions.

Emotional expression fosters transparency and open communication. When you express your emotions honestly and appropriately, you create an environment where others feel safe to do the same, leading to more productive and collaborative conversations. When you model emotional transparency, you set a positive example for your teams, fostering a culture of authenticity and trust.

Finally, emotional expression enables you to demonstrate empathy and understanding. By acknowledging and validating the emotions of others, you show that you care about your team members' well-being and are committed to supporting them. This emotional support can boost morale, engagement, and loyalty, because team members feel valued and appreciated [1].

OVERCOMING BARRIERS TO EMOTIONAL EXPRESSIONS

Many leaders hesitate to express emotion because they fear appearing vulnerable. Many of my clients believed that showing emotions, particularly those perceived as "weak," such as sadness or anxiety, can undermine their authority and credibility. This fear can lead to a suppression of emotions, even when expressing them could be beneficial for building trust and connection with their team.

Organisational cultures and expectations are another significant barrier. In today's competitive environment, many organisations have an unspoken rule that leaders should maintain a composed and unemotional demeanour. This expectation can create an environment where emotional expression is discouraged, and leaders feel they must conform to these norms to be seen as effective and competent.

Many clients also fear that expressing their emotions can be seen as a loss of control, which can be particularly concerning in high-stakes or crisis situations. The belief that emotional expression equates to a loss of control can lead to suppressing emotions, even when doing so could be detrimental to decision-making and effective communication.

Cultural and societal norms, including gender stereotypes, also play a role. Norms often dictate what emotions are acceptable, especially in professional settings. In many cultures, particularly those with a strong emphasis on stoicism and professionalism, emotional expression is seen as unprofessional or inappropriate. Leaders may feel constrained by these norms and thus suppress their emotions to maintain a perceived sense of appropriateness.

Expressing your emotions appropriately will strengthen your impact as a leader. In fact, emotional expression will help you live a healthier and happier life.

Emotions are indicators of what's happening inside ourselves. For example, anger may indicate that your boundaries are violated; sadness may indicate a sense of loss or a need for connection; fear may indicate a need for reassurance.

When emotions are suppressed instead of being fully experienced, they do not just go away. You may be able to act like you are okay and carry on with your work. Some people abuse substances such as alcohol or drugs or work all the time as a way to stuff their emotions, and over time addiction develops. Unfortunately, your body will register these suppressed emotions and start an internal countdown clock. Emotions are energy. When the energy is suppressed, it will reach an explosion point, and your health will suffer when this bomb goes off, presenting as a certain dis-ease. (See Chapter 3 under "Break free from dis-ease.")

Being able to express your emotions appropriately is the result of living your life fully and healthily; that is, experiencing emotions fully, not just the positive emotions but the negative emotions, too.

Leaders who speak with emotion are not only influential but also charismatic, a characteristic many clients come to me to develop. Charismatic leaders exude a certain aura, or presence, that attracts people and helps them make connections and be influential. Bill Clinton is often noted for his charisma, which significantly attributed to his ability to speak with emotion. His skill in connecting with audiences on an emotional level was a key factor in his political success. Clinton's speeches are known for his empathy, passion, and authenticity, making listeners feel understood and engaged. This emotional resonance helped him build rapport and trust, making his messages more impactful and memorable.

DEVELOPING EMOTIONAL EXPRESSION

If logical left brain thinking has dominated your life, we'll start with simple steps to help you develop your emotional expression.

Step 1: Observe and record your emotions.

All humans experience emotions. You may not pay attention to your emotions or you may suppress them.

Prepare a notebook and call it your Emotional Bank. The next time you experience an emotion, write it down. You can start with emotions that make an impression on you; that is, those that don't go away despite your effort to ignore them and carry on with your work.

Step 2: Observe and record where you feel the emotion in your body.

Emotions happen in the body. (See Chapter 3 under "Break free from dis-ease.") For example, when you feel fearful, this may feel like "butterflies in the stomach." People who worry a lot tend to have more stomach issues, like indigestion, than those who don't worry as much.

Record where the emotion resides physically in your body and the sensations that you experience in your body when you feel a certain emotion. For example, where is the sensation in your body when you are joyful? For me, it's a tickling sensation in my chest. Where do you feel anger in your body? It could be heaviness on your chest, together with fast and shallow breaths. Where do you feel sadness or disappointment in your body? It could be a sinking heaviness in the stomach with long and slow breaths.

On the one hand, recording the sensations you feel in your body can help you fully experience the emotion and resolve the tension there, which is a healthy way to manage and let go of negative emotions. On the other hand, the next time you have difficulty expressing a specific emotion, you can activate the sensation in the part of your body that corresponds to that emotion and you will find it easier to feel and express that emotion. Mind and body are one. When you activate the part of your body that corresponds to a certain emotion, you will feel that emotion.

Over time, when you want to express certain emotions, you won't need first to activate your bodily sensations. Expressing your emotions will become automatic.

Step 3: Practice the emotions.

With steps 1 and 2, you became more familiar with your emotions, and hopefully more at peace with them, including your negative emotions.

Use the following exercises to practice expressing different emotions. We'll focus on emotions that are often expressed in business settings.

Determination

When was the last time you felt determined? Where did you feel this in your body?

Determination is more likely to reside in your pelvic area as a feeling of heaviness. When you are determined, you are rooted and grounded.

If it is hard for you to feel the sensations in your body, you can use your breath to help you. Have you noticed that you breathe differently when experiencing different emotions? Every emotion comes with different ways of breathing. When you are angry, your breath is shallow and fast. When you feel peaceful, your breath is long and slow.

When you are determined, your breath is strong, especially on the key word(s) that help convey the emotion.

Try saying this sentence with determination: "The offer is final."

The keyword in this sentence could be "final." You'll use a stronger breath on that word. Remember, that does not mean louder. If proper breathing and full resonance have become habits as discussed in Chapters 3 and 4, when expressing determination, your abdomen will automatically pull inward for a stronger voice, with the word "final" expressed firmly.

Many clients often ask, "When do I inhale?" After the word "final," you should have felt an urge to take another breath in automatically. If not, that means you didn't use enough breath for the key word and the firmness was not precisely conveyed. No wonder people couldn't feel the impact of your words. Make sure you use all the breath you have left for the key word.

Try another one: "We must hit the target." The key word could be "must," so you'll use a stronger breath here. You should then be prompted to inhale automatically. If not, use more breath on the key word. Many clients think they have used a lot of breath, but if you are not prompted to take another inhalation automatically, that means you aren't using enough breath. Here's where you will find recording yourself helpful.

You might be wondering, "Isn't this emphasis?" In a way, yes. You are emphasising the key word by using more breath to convey determination. Focusing on the use of breath helps you to activate the emotion, and the emotional impact can be felt by the audience. Simply emphasising the word may not activate the emotion, and it tends to stay in the logical brain – yours and the audience's.

Interestingly, when clients use more breath to convey determination in the voice, they feel the difference in the mind; that is, they indeed felt more determined. Mind and body *are* one.

Using more breath on the key word does not mean saying the word louder or with a higher pitch, which can come across as irritating, demanding, or a loss of control. Using more breath also helps you convey gravitas. Being louder doesn't.

A question many clients often asked is, "Do I have to think about which word is the key word before I speak?" No, you don't. That's not practical. When you speak, your focus is on how well the audience is receiving your message. That focus will direct you to decide which word you want them to remember as you speak.

If it is challenging to decide what the key word is as you speak, you can do daily practices of finding the key words in sentences that you often need to say at work and practicing different emotions. Or find any paragraph in a book or magazine or newspaper for practice. We'll practice that in the next section.

Empathy/caring

To convey empathy, the breath is long and slow on the keyword.

For example, "I understand your situation." Your breath will be long and slow on the keyword "understand".

Does this mean elongating the word? No. Remember, your focus is on your breath. It is the breath that activates the emotion. When you focus on elongating the word, you don't feel the emotion and what you say has no impact. Instead, focus on breathing out slowly on the word "understand," specifically the key syllable "stand," and you'll feel the emotion.

You'll also notice when you feel empathy that your volume decreases as you say "your situation." See Figure 5.1 showing the volume change.

On another note, reflection, though not an emotion, is worth highlighting here. In the last chapter, we talked about "pause for reflection." Giving your audience time for reflection is essential, because people are only influenced when they have time to reflect on how what they've heard applies to their own lives. You'll not only pause but also need to deliver the sentence in a way that invites people to reflect. Voice for reflection is similar to voice for empathy.

For example, "What are the consequences if you continue with the same behaviour?" On the word "continue," your breath will be long and slow, and then your volume will decrease, ending the sentence with a downward inflection followed by a pause to invite people to reflect.

Take note on the use of downward inflection to end the sentence. Upward inflection invites answers to the question, which is not the

Figure 5.1 Volume change indication when expressing empathy.

purpose for reflection. Rhetorical questions are used for reflection and do not require a verbal answer.

We need a quiet environment for reflection; therefore, your volume should be quieter. Use your voice to create an environment of reflection for your audience, rather than saying, "Now reflect on ...."

Curiosity

Do you know you can speak for long hours without ever losing your voice?

In the last chapter, we talked about "pause for suspense." Suspense or curiosity is the cornerstone to keeping people engaged. Not only will you pause before the punch line but you will deliver the entire sentence in a way that piques people's curiosity.

Speaking with curiosity in your voice requires having fun with what you say. Many clients have rejected this idea: "Oh, no, no, no. My work requires seriousness." In my work with corporate professionals, I've noticed that 95% of them are way too serious. Yes, business is serious, which is why we spent a whole chapter talking about gravitas! But this mindset has resulted in people becoming so serious and stressed out that they don't know how to have fun anymore.

"How did this happen?" A client asked me. "I couldn't even think of any funny experience to use as a story."

"The body expresses what the mind represses." Not only has stress made people dull but stress shows up in the voice. Many clients have tension in their voices, sounding restricted or closed up. Remember, we also talked about the importance of levity in the last chapter.

To have fun while speaking with curiosity, think about how fun it is to work with how the human brain functions – to be more specific, how our attention functions. We give our attention to things we are curious about.

I use the sentence at the beginning of this section when I speak to audiences who need to speak for long hours yet often lose their voices. Right after saying the sentence, I always hear someone in the audience ask, "How?" That's when you know they are curious.

Practice saying the sentence while feeing light-hearted and teasing people as if you know something they don't, with a sense of mystery, as if you were to reveal a secret to them, and pause after the words "without ever" long enough before the punch line "losing your voice".

Record your practice. Listen to the recording and think about what your response would be if you were the listener. Would your response be, "Yes, tell me more!" or "Oh, okay." If the latter, you didn't pique their curiosity. When practicing, exaggerate your voice and expression to train your expressive muscles.

Excitement

When you feel excited, you may notice sensations in your chest. Activate the sensation and try saying the sentence, "We have an exciting year ahead!" You may notice that your pitch was higher and your volume increased. This doesn't work the other way around, though. If you just raise your voice to express excitement, you will sound inauthentic.

You'll need to keep one thing in mind. If you have made proper breathing and full resonance habits based on the practices in the last two chapters, when your voice pitch rises, your voice is still fully resonant, not sharp or shrill, which pushes people away.

Anger

Many clients have asked me, "How do I convey seriousness when I'm angry without sounding like I'm losing control?" This is what we want to talk about regarding expressing anger – appropriately.

Anger is an emotion that many people, including the old me, want to avoid or suppress. Like all other emotions, anger signals what happens at an unconscious level. For example, it could be that your boundaries are being violated or it could be fear that makes you put up fences so others will stay away. By acknowledging anger and channeling the energy appropriately, you can identify the real problem and find effective solutions.

One way to help you channel anger's energy properly and sound in control and composed while still expressing the seriousness of the matter is using all your breath, or energy, on the keyword.

For example, try the sentence: "How could you do that?" Use all your breath on one word. The word you choose determines the message you want to convey. Let's try the word "how." Remember, when using all of your breath, you should notice your abdomen moving inward automatically, and after the word "how" you should automatically be prompted to inhale.

When most people are angry their voice gets higher pitched. A high pitch conveys a loss of control and causes people to put up their defences and resist. Using all of your breath on a keyword lowers your pitch down and conveys more seriousness.

These are the five major emotions my clients express in business: determination, empathy/caring, curiosity, excitement, and anger. You can use the same process to express other emotions such as pride, hope, disappointment, etc.; that is, activating the sensations in the body or using your breath on keywords.

Many clients have lamented, "My normal day-to-day speaking voice doesn't convey any emotion." That is a misconception. Even if you start your meeting with "Good morning," you can sound welcoming or inviting. Speaking with emotions needs to become a habit. You need to train your muscles to be expressive. When it becomes a habit, you'll find everything you say conveys a certain emotion. Yes, even when reporting the numbers. Did the number increase? Was the increase surprising? Or did it bring a sense of urgency or reassurance? Look beyond the black words on white paper.

EXERCISES: SPEAK WITH EMOTIONS

Exercise 1

"In the early years of the company, every new employee was given a blanket and a mattress. During their lunch break at noon, they would take a nap – both convenient and practical."

This paragraph looks factual at first glance. If you read it carefully, were you curious: Why were they given a blanket and a mattress? If you were not curious, work on your curiosity. Curiosity is what keeps us young and alive!

> "We don't stop playing because we grow old; we grow old because we stop playing."
>
> – George Bernard Shaw

Imagine you need to elicit curiosity in your audience. Have fun with how people's brains and attention work. Deliver this exercise's opening sentence with curiosity and mystery, especially on the words "blanket" and "mattress," because those are the items people will be wondering about.

The next sentence is where you reveal the why. Aha, because they used them to take a nap on! So the word "nap" is the big reveal and you'll deliver it with a sense of "aha!"

Now you see, with the two sentences, we've already expressed emotions, and the emotions form a melody, pulling people's attention in, raising it up and then coming down as we reveal it with a big "aha." Many clients have said, "I want to have melody when I speak." That's how you have it. It's not by varying your voice pitch, pace, tone, or volume, which is technical. Techniques disconnect you from people's emotions and leave no impact. It is feeling the emotions and expressing the emotions that lead to a beautiful and touching melody.

Exercise 2

The following excerpt is from Winston Churchill's speech "We Shall Fight on the Beaches":

> "You ask, what is our aim? I can answer in one word: victory – victory at all costs, victory in spite of all terror, victory, however long and hard the road may be; for without victory, there is no survival."

The key emotion in this paragraph is determination. On the words "one" and the first "victory," you'll need to speak with determination. The following three instances of "victory" are an escalation of the emotion. Keep in mind the rule of three. If you want to escalate emotions, construct three sentences that share similar structures or repeat a keyword in three sentences. This turbo charges the impact.

To escalate the determination here, use stronger and faster breath with each sentence. You'll notice your volume and your pace increase. On the last part of the sentence, "for without victory, there is no survival," the voice pitch lowers so people can reflect, with a long and slow breath on the keywords "without" and "no."

For this paragraph, the voice also ends up with a melodic delivery due to the change of emotions. Many clients have found they felt so much determination and conviction as their breath and voice changed. Mind and body are indeed one.

Many clients have shared, "Oh, I would love to see how Churchill delivered the speech." Yes, it is helpful to see how he delivered it. But don't imitate how he did it or you'll remain at the technique level. Go inward to feel determined and deliver the speech.

Exercise 3

"A change in pitch on the boat they were following knifed through his sorrow. Immediately, he cut the engine on the runabout, listened to the sea and the night. The night was now very dark as the storm clouds continued to overrun the starlight."

Stories provide some of the best material for learning to speak with emotions. Stories are filled with emotional twists and turns. Stories also elicit pictures in people's minds, which helps to engage them and makes what you say more memorable.

For this story, the key note is quietness – quietness for the character's sorrow and for the darkness on the sea. Therefore, your volume will be quiet. How beautifully it is written: "listened to the sea and the night." Express it similarly to how you would ask people to reflect, with your volume becoming quieter and quieter as you speak, letting people visualise the scene in their minds.

There is also some intensity, indicated by the words "knifed through" and "cut." Express these words with intensity. Good writing is done using contrast. There is quietness and there is intensity. There is sorrow yet the pitch change slaps the face of the sorrow. The story is filled with twists and turns; though trying to be quiet, danger is on the horizon, or never disappeared but temporarily absent. Such good writing facilitates the melodic delivery through your voice.

Many clients have asked, "Do I have to analyse my emotions before speaking?" The answer is no. The exercises listed here are for practice purposes and for training your expressive muscles. You want to find stories, speeches, etc., to practice, and you will analyse these in practices. Ultimately, you want emotional expression to become part of you. Then over time, you will find that you've become an engaging speaker who leaves an impact.

CRAFTING AND DELIVERING EMOTIONALLY ENGAGING AND INSPIRING TALKS

The three exercises above demonstrate not only how to speak with emotions but also how critical it is to craft your talks to be emotionally engaging and inspiring in the first place.

Yes, your presentations or talks might have facts, numbers, and data to tell. But to get buy-in for your suggestions or proposals and get people to take action, emotion is essential. After all, logic makes people think and emotion makes people act.

Here are some general ideas and strategies to incorporate into your talks.

Understand what matters to people

What are the challenges people are going through? What are their aspirations? What motivates them? What are their fears? What keeps them up at night?

Tailor your talks to address their specific challenges, needs, and emotions to connect with them on a deep emotional level, so they know you understand them and may have the solutions to their challenges.

Express pain and pleasure

Pain and pleasure are fundamental human emotional motivators. When you speak, highlight the potential loss or consequences that might occur if no action is taken. This can result in a desire to find solutions and a sense of urgency towards action.

Though we are more motivated by the fear of losing something than by the prospect of gaining something new, it is appealing to emphasise the benefits and rewards of a particular action.

Use a combination of pain and pleasure to create a balanced and compelling argument. For example, "By adopting this proposal, we'll avoid the potential loss by 20% and enjoy the certainty and peace of mind."

This is where understanding what matters to the people you are talking to is a pre-requisite. If the pain and pleasure you discuss do not matter much to your audience, your words will have no impact on them.

Use emotional language

Choose vivid and descriptive words when you want to evoke emotions: words that appeal to the senses of sight, sound, touch, taste, and smell. This helps people visualise and feel your message more deeply. Instead of saying, "The beach was nice," say, "The beach was a breathtaking vista of golden sands and azure waters, with the soothing sound of waves gently lapping against the shore."

If you tend to speak in a logical way, perhaps the change for you to make is embracing metaphors and analogies. They help make complex ideas more relatable and emotionally resonant. Zen masters are masters of metaphors. When disciples come to them with complex issues, the masters do not use logic to convince them. They say, "Look at the clouds . . ." or "Look at the water .... " Their use of metaphor will help you cut through the noise and see clearly what the root of your problem is. The next time when you want to explain a complex issue, think about what metaphor or analogy you can use.

Employ tools such as rhetorical questions, escalation of emotion using the rule of three, and contrast discussed in the three exercises presented earlier.

Tell stories

"Using words to explain words"

Fillip wanted to talk about the importance of self-care with his team. He wrote in his speech, "Self-care is important, because self-care can help prevent various health issues, including chronic diseases such as heart disease and diabetes. Self-care also boosts the immune system, making the body more resilient to infections and illnesses. Engaging in self-care activities can increase energy levels, helping you feel more alert and productive throughout the day."

"No one will remember that, or they don't even bother to listen," I said frankly. "You are using words to explain words. It won't stay in people's mind. It can also come across as preaching." I was curious: "How did you come to the conclusion that self-care is important? I've not heard that often from a man!"

"Well, it was because of my sister." He shared, "Recently she had health issues and had to be hospitalised. That's where she realised the importance of self-care."

"Why don't you share that story?" I asked. "Use the story to relate the importance of self-care. And put all the benefits of self-care in the story as the character's words."

Fillip did just that. He was happy to hear from some team members later, "I learned about the importance of self-care because of my mom's health issues."

Using more words to explain a point is a common mistake. You'll lose your audience's attention and come across as preaching. The next time you want to make a point, ask yourself, "Which story can I use to illustrate this point?" And, of course, start collecting stories!

Manchester United

Gavin wanted to inspire his staff to never give up. I asked him to think about a personal story that demonstrated this spirit. In the next session, he suggested a story of Manchester United. "I couldn't think of a personal story, so I wanted to use a story from my favourite football team."

"What about the Liverpool fans in your staff? They may not want to listen to you," I joked. "Besides, the Manchester United story you're thinking of is well known. Before you even finish telling the story, they will know how it ends. Of course you have your own stories. I'm sure that in advancing your career to the C-suite, you have many stories that demonstrate this spirit of never giving up." I asked Gavin to find a personal story or even stories from his team that demonstrated that spirit.

When Gavin came back for the next session, he had found his own story.

To start your story collection, dedicate another notebook called Story Bank. Whenever something memorable happens, write a few keywords to help you remember the story, and give the story a name so both you and the audience can easily refer to it.

Think of the points you often need to get across to your team or staff; for example, never give up, think outside the box, be resilient, etc. Start collecting stories to animate these motivations.

Be authentic

We talked about the importance of authenticity earlier. To speak with authenticity, share lessons you've learned, including failures and struggles. That's why I strongly recommended that Gavin find his own story. Vulnerability makes you human and relatable, able to connect with people emotionally.

Perfection is an illusion. When you present yourself as perfect, people sense that this is unreal, which can create distance between you.

"You are too perfect."

Josephine has aways presented herself as flawless; it showed in how she looked and how she spoke. She was even scouted for an audition while walking on the street. She told me, "My colleagues and team respect me, but there's a gap I don't seem to bridge in trying to get closer to them. I wonder if it has to do with my voice?"

"Can I be honest with you?" I asked.

"Sure. That's what I'm here for."

"You are too perfect. Perfection creates distance."

"But I've only been trying to be appropriate. Is that wrong?" She was confused.

"What would happen if you were not appropriate?"

As our conversation deepened, she shared her experience of growing up in a country she was not born in and how she felt she had to look appropriate and speak appropriately in order to be accepted.

"Have you accepted yourself, fully, including all the so-called flaws and imperfections?" I asked.

To be authentic, a key step is working on accepting yourself fully. How you perceive yourself is how others will respond to you. When you try to hide your flaws and imperfections, people will unconsciously wait for the other shoe to drop, anticipating that something will go wrong eventually. Imperfection is perfect. You want to improve yourself not because you are not perfect but because you want to become better or more effective at doing your job. Intention matters in your desire for improvement.

To speak with an authentic voice, search inward to see how you authentically feel. In trying to sound determined, for example, search inward and see where the sensations are when you feel determined. A client shared, "Okay, I see Churchill's volume was stronger when he was determined. I want to adopt that voice." No. Stop trying to sound like Churchill. We don't need another Churchill. We need YOU.

Turn narration into conversation

This is one of the most powerful yet most overlooked delivery tools. Most people narrate when they speak. It is very linear, which doesn't keep people's attention.

For example: "John told me he would not be able to finish the project on time." Your audience's response would probably be, "Okay." We talked about that earlier – "Okay" will not grab or keep their attention.

Instead, turn narration into a conversation: "John told me, 'I won't be able to finish the project on time.'"

Once John starts "talking," you can use whatever persona or emotion that suits John. Perhaps John is a loud speaker, or he is feeling sorry, or he is frustrated. Turning narration into a conversation makes John come alive and become memorable.

To speak to be engaging and inspiring, you need to work on crafting a talk that's emotionally engaging and inspiring as well as on the delivery.

HOW TO SPEAK WITH CONVICTION

Conviction is a firm and strongly held belief or opinion. It is rooted in personal values, principles, and emotions. It goes beyond just knowing something. It involves a commitment to that belief and a willingness to stand by it, even in the face of opposition. A leader who speaks with conviction is not easily swayed by opposing views or doubts. It is not just being assertive; there is an unwavering confidence about one's own thoughts and ideas. That can inspire respect and trust from people.

Speaking with certainty, discussed in the chapter on gravitas, refers to a state of being completely sure about something, often based on evidence, facts, or logical reasoning. It is about the intellectual or cognitive aspect of knowing that something is true or will happen. For example, we have certainty that the sun will rise tomorrow based on astronomical evidence, unless the weather doesn't cooperate, but we can't say that we have conviction that the sun will rise tomorrow.

Conviction has a strong emotional component. It requires you to develop genuine, unwavering confidence about a belief or opinion that you stand by. To deliver your words with conviction, use the skills you have acquired so far, including:

1. Speaking with a fully resonant voice that projects gravitas
2. Speaking with emotion, especially determination
3. Speaking with authenticity
4. Understanding and addressing what matters to people

   There is one more skill to add to emphasise your conviction:
5. Gesturing on keywords

Gesture on the capitalised keywords in the following: "I can answer in ONE word: VICTORY."

Try using a strong fist or an open sideways-facing palm to show strength as you say the key words. The key is to convey your conviction with firmness.

Your words and your gestures must be in sync. When they are, you may notice that your gestures significantly enhance your voice delivery.

Speaking with conviction amplifies your impact and transforms the way you connect and inspire people. In addition to mastering the skills we've discussed, a deep understanding of your subject is fundamental, developed through investing time researching and comprehending the core elements of your topic.

> "People hear you on your level of consciousness."
>
> – Marianne Williamson

The more you know and the higher you elevate yourself, the more confidently you can speak, and this confidence is palpable.

COMPASSION

"I wish to hold an umbrella over you, for I, too, have been caught in the storm."

This Chinese quote (因为我曾淋过雨，所以想为你撑把伞) perfectly explains compassion.

Compassion is beyond "I put myself in your shoes and understand what you are going through, though I myself may or may not have gone through that experience or the feelings."

Compassion is "Yes, I've been through the experience or the feelings that you are going through, and I understand personally the struggle, the suffering, the pain, the desperation, or the hopelessness. Therefore, I am here to help alleviate your suffering."

That's the difference between empathy and compassion. Compassion comes from a place of loving kindness and, in Buddhism, is essential on the path to enlightenment. Empathy is not a step on the path to enlightenment. Empathy is the first step. The ultimate state is compassion. Compassion and wisdom are two wings of a bird, both necessary on the path to enlightenment, because they purify the mind from negative emotions such as greed, hatred, and ignorance, which are the source of suffering.

In Christianity, compassion is deeply rooted in the concept of love. One of the most famous teachings on compassion in Christianity is the Parable of the Good Samaritan (Luke 10:25–37). In this story, Jesus illustrates compassion through the actions of a Samaritan who helps a wounded man, despite cultural and religious differences. In the Sermon on the Mount, Jesus outlines the Beatitudes, which include blessings for those who show mercy and compassion (Matthew 5:7). This teaching highlights the spiritual rewards of being compassionate and merciful.

In Islam, compassion is closely tied to the concept of mercy, as demonstrated by the life of the Prophet Muhammad, who serves as a model of compassion, and the practices of *Zakat* ("charity") and *Sadaqah* ("voluntary charity").

In all religions and spiritual practices, compassion, not empathy, is the path to transforming suffering, cultivating positive qualities, and progressing towards a more enlightened state of being.

How does compassion relate to you as a business leader?

Compassion, not empathy, has become one of the top qualities people want to see in a leader, especially in recent years of crisis and chaos [2]. Compassionate leaders are proven to foster trust, loyalty, and engagement among their employees [3, 4].

Speaking with compassion can't be cultivated using techniques. Compassion is a practice and cultivation of the heart.

"If you are going through hell, keep going." This is how you cultivate compassion – well, one of the ways. It was through the experience of being bullied at work, living in fear, and feeling voiceless that I gained a profound understanding of the struggles of those who go unheard and whose voices are suppressed. This journey led me to discover my own voice and, ultimately, to find my mission to help you find your voice.

It was through the experience of starting my business in a foreign country without connection and financial support, waking up in the middle of the night in a cold sweat wondering where my next client was that I learned to understand and relate to those who live in uncertainty and anxiety, those who must face their fears head on, and those who pursue their dreams with unshakable faith.

It was through the experience of facing broken commitments in a relationship that I tasted the excruciating pain of helplessness and hopelessness, bringing me to my knees, eventually pushing me to rise. This experience helped me build heartfelt connections with those whose hearts are shattered into pieces and then stomped on over and over again, those who are in despair when being surrounded in total darkness, and those who endure seemingly insurmountable suffering and are brought to their knees.

If I had not seen the darkness, if I had not gone to rock bottom, if I had not faced the demons, how would I be able to tell you exactly what darkness, rock bottom, and demons look like, feel like, and taste like? Sure, I could tell you what I read in books or saw on TV, but this is left brain knowledge that'll stay in your head, and will never touch your heart.

"What is to give light must endure burning." – Viktor E. Frankl.

I wish you didn't need to experience any suffering in life to learn compassion. Unfortunately, that's not how life is designed. We all go through suffering. Some don't want to admit it or aren't even aware! You either just survived suffering, or are currently suffering, or are going to experience suffering. Since we are all going to go through suffering, why not fully experience it, rise from it, and become a more compassionate person? "The phoenix must burn to emerge" (Janet Fitch).

When you emerge, you'll relate to people in a deep and profound way. Not only will you become a better leader but, most importantly, you'll become a better human being.

REFERENCES

[1] Ashkanasy, N. M., and Dorris, C. S. (2002). "Emotions in the Workplace." *Annual Reviews*, 4, 67–90.

[2] Nielsen, N. C., Auria, G. D., and Zolley, S. (2020). "What Are You Feeling?" McKinsey Insights. https://www.mckinsey.com/capabilities/people-and-organizational-performance/our-insights/tuning-in-turning-outward-cultivating-compassionate-leadership-in-a-crisis

[3] Dutton, J. E., Frost, P. J., Worline, M. C., Lilius, J. M., and Kanov, J. M. (2002). "Leading in Times of Trauma." *Harvard Business Review*, 80(1), 54–61.

[4] Powley, E. H., and Piderit, S. K. (2008). "Trending Wounds: Elements of the Organizational Healing Process." *Journal of Applied Behavioural Science*, 44(1), 134–149.

Leadership voice quality – Equanimity

Six

"Stillness is where creativity and solutions to problems are found."
– Eckhart Tolle

WHAT IS EQUANIMITY?

Equanimity is a concept found in many philosophies and spiritual traditions, including Buddhism, Taoism, Stoicism, and yoga philosophy.

Equanimity is a remarkable ability to remain grounded, centred, and present, regardless of what's happening externally. It's the ability to not get knocked off centre or be reactive even when external situations are difficult, uncertain, and chaotic, even when you are emotionally triggered and the circumstances are out of control.

Equanimity is the eye of the storm and the centre of the tornado. No matter what's going on around you, you stay internally still, calm, and peaceful. It is what sets exemplary human beings apart. It is what enables great leaders to navigate challenging situations and make better decisions with composure, calmness, and wisdom.

Here are some key characteristics of equanimity:

1. Stability: Equanimity implies a balanced and stable mind that remains steady and calm, even when faced with challenges or adversity.
2. Acceptance: It involves accepting situations as they are, rather than resisting or denying them. This is not passivity but rather the ability to acknowledge the reality of a situation before taking appropriate action.
3. Non-reactivity: People with equanimity are not easily disturbed or upset by external events. They have the capacity to respond thoughtfully, rather than react impulsively.
4. Emotional regulation: Equanimity helps in managing emotions effectively. It's not about suppressing emotions but rather about experiencing them without being overwhelmed or controlled by them.

DOI: 10.4324/9781003596486-6

5. Being present: Equanimity involves being present with whatever is happening, without judgement or attachment. It does not focus on the past with regret or the future with worry.
6. Wisdom: It reflects a deeper understanding and wisdom about the nature of life, including its ups and downs, and the ability to see the bigger picture.
7. Patience and tolerance: Equanimity fosters patience and tolerance, towards both oneself and others. It helps in dealing with uncertainty and frustration.
8. Inner peace: Ultimately, equanimity is about cultivating inner peace and tranquility. It's a quality that can be developed over time with practices like meditation, mindfulness, and self-reflection.

THE NEUROSCIENCE BEHIND EQUANIMITY

At the core of the brain's stress response is the amygdala, an almond-shaped structure located deep within the temporal lobe. The amygdala plays a crucial role in processing emotions, particularly fear, anxiety, and aggression. When we perceive a threat, whether real or imagined, the amygdala triggers the "fight-or-flight" response, activating the sympathetic nervous system and releasing stress hormones like cortisol and adrenaline. This response is essential for survival, but chronic activation can lead to long-term health issues, including high blood pressure, a weakened immune system, and increased risk of heart disease [1].

In contrast, the prefrontal cortex (PFC), located at the front of the brain, is involved in executive functions such as decision-making, impulse control, and emotional regulation. The PFC helps modulate the amygdala's stress response by providing a more rational and balanced perspective. When the PFC is active, it can inhibit the amygdala's reactivity, promoting a state of equanimity. This is often referred to as the "top-down" regulation of emotions, where higher-order cognitive processes influence and control lower-order emotional responses [1].

Mindfulness and meditation practices have been shown to strengthen the connection between the PFC and the amygdala, enhancing emotional regulation and resilience. For instance, mindfulness-based stress reduction programs have been found to increase gray matter density in the PFC and decrease amygdala activity. This results in improved emotional regulation, reduced stress reactivity, and enhanced overall well-being [2].

Moreover, neuroplasticity – the brain's ability to change and adapt – plays a significant role in cultivating equanimity. Regular practice of mindfulness and meditation can induce neuroplastic changes, strengthening the neural pathways associated with emotional regulation and resilience. This means that the more we practice equanimity, the more it becomes a natural and automatic response to stress and emotions [3, 4].

The neuroscience of equanimity also highlights the importance of the parasympathetic nervous system, which is responsible for the "rest and digest" response. Activating the parasympathetic nervous system through practices like deep breathing, relaxation techniques, and gentle yoga can counteract the stress response, promoting a state of calm and balance. This activation helps reduce the heart rate, lower blood pressure, and decrease muscle tension, further enhancing equanimity [5].

VOICES THAT LACK EQUANIMITY

Voice reflects everything about you. All of your issues, whether physical, mental, or emotional, show up in your voice.

The following are a few examples of voices that lack equanimity.

- A trembling voice
  Often when people are nervous, their voice may tremble or they may speak at a higher pitch or a faster pace. As mentioned in the chapter on gravitas, for some clients, the voice may tremble when they are not nervous as well.

  Regardless, a voice that trembles reflects the fight-or-flight response. If your voice trembles when you are not nervous, this could be an indication that you are regularly in fight-or-flight mode; that is, constantly worrying about the worst-case scenario.
- Vocal fry
  Vocal fry refers to a voice that's not supported by breath and sounds much like the sizzling sound on a frying pan. It's as if your voice was being squeezed out of your throat.

  Vocal fry indicates a feeling that you don't have the right to speak. This could be due to your upbringing, where you were not encouraged to speak, often told to shut up or to be seen but not heard, or your ideas were often rejected, and so on. As a result of these experiences, you've dimmed your light, minimising your presence.

- A voice that suppresses stress/emotions
  A person with equanimity does not suppress stress or emotions but experiences these feelings without being overwhelmed or controlled by them. When you suppress stress and emotions, it can be heard in the voice as unclear, soft, or even muffled. Your voice won't be able to project very far and you'll feel breathless after speaking for some time.
- A withheld voice
  A withheld voice is the result of holding your breath while trying to speak. We talked about this in the chapter on space. Breath is our life force. When you hold your breath while speaking, you are holding back your life force, your vitality. You also have no exchange with the people and world around you, because breath is how we make exchanges with what's around us. You are withholding yourself from interacting with others and the environment.

  When I was travelling in Hawaii a few years ago, I learned that in the Hawaiian language, the word *aloha* serves as a greeting, expressing love, affection, and peace. Its literal meaning is deeply profound: to exchange breaths with the person you greet. The syllable *ha* translates to "breath," underscoring the significance ancient Hawaiians placed on the breath as a sacred and genuine form of exchange. This perspective reflects the Hawaiian culture's holistic approach to communication and interpersonal connections.
- An intimidating or a fierce voice and a reactive voice
  An intimidating voice – even a loud voice – sets up an invisible wall around you that protects you from being hurt or being taken advantage of. You've learned a way to protect yourself from being vulnerable, often pushing people away.

"How do I sound more caring?"

Thomas was known for being tough throughout his career. His staff was afraid of him. When he wanted to take a back seat and encourage young leaders to speak up and step up, he realised his tough voice didn't work well.

"When I speak, they think I'm angry and are intimidated. No one dares to speak up. I need to speak in a gentler manner so they will see me as approachable and as a patient and caring advisor."

People with a tough and intimidating voice tend to be reactive as if guarding against anything that has the potential to hurt them. That's "fight" in the fight-or-flight reaction. Equanimity requires you to be non-reactive. Non-reactivity results from your inner work on becoming comfortable with displaying your vulnerability. "In my defencelessness, my safety lies" (Marianne Williamson). Vulnerability is the ultimate strength.

- A voice that tries to fit in

  If you need to feel accepted, or are constantly seeking validation, or are often uncertain of what you say – or even if you can switch among different accents depending on whom you are speaking to – all of these can be heard in the voice as trying to fit in.

  You might be thinking, "How can you even hear all that in the voice?" Well, you can. Remember: voice reflects everything about you. Most people can unconsciously sense these differences, even if they can't quite put their finger on what exactly it is that's different.

  Voice is basically vibration supported by breath. The way you use your breath changes how your voice comes across. For example, a person with a pleasing voice could be using too much breath while a withheld voice doesn't use enough breath. And how the voice vibrates or where it vibrates changes how the voice comes across, too.

  Developing equanimity can help you build an inner unshakable core that will keep you grounded and centred with being who you are. You will accept who you are regardless of how others perceive you. The world around us responds to us just as we respond to ourselves. As the saying goes, "We teach others how to treat us." When you accept yourself, you'll notice that others accept you as well. And for those who don't – ignore them. That's their own problem to deal with.
- An arrogant voice

  An arrogant voice implies a sense of superiority. It's heard in the way the breath is used. The breath is lighter and the pitch is higher at the end of sentences.

  Superiority is a facade to compensate for one's inadequacy, insecurity, and inferiority. It can work as a shield to avoid being criticised. People who feel superior are looking for external validation to gain respect and admiration. True security comes from accepting and loving the whole you, not just some parts. When you make peace with yourself, you make peace with everyone and everything around you.

- An inauthentic voice

  In the chapter on emotion we talked about a client who tried to sound like Winston Churchill when trying to speak with determination. That's an example of an inauthentic voice – using a certain voice that you think will be accepted or appropriate that doesn't align with how you really feel or think. There's a disconnection between how you authentically feel and think and how you think you should sound.

  It's like thinking, "You want an inspirational voice? Let me give you an inspirational voice. I'll speak loudly with big gestures, and I'll make my voice go up and down so it's not monotonous." Yes, it sounds like a performance. "I am performing what you want to hear." This is perceived as fake and doesn't allow people to see the real you. It might be that you don't even know who you authentically are, so you avoid looking inward, afraid that you will find nothing.

- A breathy voice

  A breathy voice sounds like a sigh, breathing out more than breathing in. Breath is our life force. When you lose your life force, you sound and feel tired. We sigh when we feel disappointed. A person with a breathy voice could be disappointed with their own life compared to others: "Look at John and Jane. They've got everything. Poor me."

  Interesting, isn't it? Your voice shows the world what's happening inside of you, even on an unconscious level. How do you find out what's happening inside? Record yourself often and listen to the recording. Or work with me.

- A monotonous voice

  A monotonous voice can be due to many factors. Are you too logical? Is your thinking too linear? Has your right brain (emotions) been well developed? (See the chapter on emotions.) Do you use one type of voice – for example, cheerful or excited – all the time? Some clients who are professional speakers speak in a high-pitched, pumped-up voice for the entire speech thinking that's inspiring. It is not inspiring – it's monotonous and can be irritating. Our ears can't hear a high-pitched voice for too long.

  "My monotone keeps people calm," a participant in a workshop shared. A voice that keeps people calm comes from a place in you that's grounded, centred, and unwavering; in other words, equanimity, which does not equal to monotone, the equivalent of being boring and dull.

- A floating voice
  A floating voice sounds airy, as if coming from the head. It's not grounded. It gives people the impression that you are not down to earth but constantly chasing the next shiny object. You live too much in your head, with thoughts running all over the place at all times. There's a disconnection in your body and from your body. Try to observe yourself and your thoughts, coming and going. That's one way to practice equanimity.
- An indifferent voice
  An indifferent voice sounds disengaged and disassociated from people, as if there was an invisible gap between you and others. It keeps people away, and they may see you as aloof. An indifferent voice can also come across as monotonous.

  When you speak with equanimity, you will not sound indifferent. An indifferent voice keeps you from being disturbed by disengaging, whereas equanimity allows you to engage and experience without being disturbed or overwhelmed. Equanimity is a remarkable quality that sets exemplary human beings apart. Indeed, it is one of the Four Immeasurables (Brahmavihārā) in Buddhism (*upekkhā* in Sanskrit), along with loving-kindness (*mettā*), sympathetic joy (*muditā*), and compassion (*karunā*), all of which are necessary on your path to enlightenment.
- A pre-occupied voice
  We are living in a world where we are constantly bombarded with information and distractions. Together with stress, anxiety, and a diminished ability to focus, we are pulled further and further away from being in the present. When the mind is pre-occupied, it is reflected in the voice. Many people only engage their head to speak and project their voices. They are not living in the body. When you are not living in your body, as a leader, how can you stay present and genuinely engage people?

DEVELOPING A VOICE OF EQUANIMITY

"I felt so calm when I was being challenged"

Jane spoke in her company's cross-function meetings regularly. When she made a proposal or expressed her opinions, she was often challenged. She would get very upset and her voice pitch would go up. She said, "I believe that made me lose all credibility and people just didn't want to listen anymore."

As her voice work progressed, she noted, "In recent meetings, I was still challenged, but I felt so calm. This is so surprising."

Many clients were surprised that after working on transforming their voices, they felt calmer.

That is the power of a full voice, a voice that resonates fully in your body. To achieve your full voice, we've talked about proper breathing in the chapter on space and activating your chest cavity and developing full resonance in the body in the chapter on gravitas.

Proper breathing, or diaphragmatic breathing, can inhibit the amygdala's reactivity, reducing the intensity of emotional responses and promoting a more balanced state of mind. It can also enhance the activity of the PFC, allowing for better emotional regulation and more rational decision-making under stress. Furthermore, diaphragmatic breathing stimulates the parasympathetic nervous system, which is responsible for the body's "rest and digest" functions, and lowers cortisol levels, the body's primary stress hormone, helping to reduce stress and promote relaxation [6]. The key here is that diaphragmatic breathing must become a habit. Only then will you be able to become less reactive and calm, even during times of stress.

Activation and full resonance help ground and centre you. The chest cavity, as the largest sound resonance chamber, once activated, grounds your voice in the full body. When you feel tense, nervous, or emotionally turbulent, your voice will not tremble or shake but will instead sound calm. Mind and body are one. When your voice sounds calm, you will feel calm.

I'm continuously amazed at how powerful the full voice is. I was traveling in the United States a few years ago and had a rental car. One night in a new city, I parked the car in a district where the crime rate was high. I hadn't done any research on the safety of the district until I arrived there. You know the feeling where you can instinctively sense how unsafe a place is? That's what happened. Unfortunately, I had booked a hotel in the area. I parked the car two blocks away from the hotel because I couldn't find a parking lot nearby. When I checked in, I found the hotel had secure parking. I walked back to the car, but it wasn't there! My stomach sank and I felt a chill running down my spine. "Oh, my god, my laptop!" It's interesting what we think is most important at times like that. "I hope the car rental insurance covers a stolen car! Where do I even report this?" I felt so panicked, yet I was walking slowly as if nothing had happened! "How could I feel so calm?!" I was shocked at my own response. I attributed this to my years of speaking with full resonance. And sometimes we do stupid things. As I walked around slowly, I suddenly realised, "I parked in the next street!" Phew! Who would have recognised the streets – they all looked the same in an unfamiliar city!

Many clients and friends often say to me, "Cynthia, you always sound so calm." But I don't always feel calm. However, speaking with a fully resonant voice is definitely a key contributor. As you work on your full voice, every step trains you to be calmer, less reactive, more stable, more grounded, and more centred. In times of panic or other emotional stress, you will have evolved to be calmer than most people.

Now you have the keys to developing a voice of equanimity; that is, a full voice or a fully resonant voice. The three steps to achieving a full voice covered in previous chapters are diaphragmatic breathing, activation, and full resonance.

Here are a few additional points to fine-tune your voice of equanimity.

- Pace

  As we discussed in the chapter on gravitas, there are times when you want to speak fast for greater impact. But, in general, a slower pace is better. A slower pace signals that you are patient, stable, accepting, and wise. If someone talking about enlightenment is speeding through their speech like a race car, you might doubt their credibility. And your doubts would be valid!

  When you rush through a speech, you are not in the moment and are rushing through life. What's the point of rushing to the finishing line of your life only to realise you haven't really lived each moment?

  "You don't understand," many clients have said. "I have so much to do in so little time. I have people I'm responsible for." Well, who doesn't?

  There's a Chinese saying, 欲速则不达, meaning the more you rush, the further away you are from your destination. Clarity, focus, and patience will get you where you intend to go.
- Use of breath

  One way the lack of equanimity is revealed is through the way you use your breath. How fast or slowly do you breathe out when speaking? Do you even use your breath when speaking? Do you use too much breath when speaking? Is your breathing light or heavy? Do you have consistent breath in your speech? Do you feel breathless? Is your breath supporting your voice projection? Becoming more aware of how you use your breath when speaking is the first step to transformation. The next step is using diaphragmatic breathing habitually. And the last step is using your breath well. When you are speaking, breath is supposed to flow out smoothly; when you are expressing different emotions, your breath varies accordingly, as we discussed in the chapter on emotions.

- Grounding and centring practice

  Many people in today's world are living in their own heads, preoccupied with their own thoughts, worries, and internal narratives, not focused on the present and connection with people around them. As a result, when they speak, they are all over the place, or they don't even remember what they wanted to get across, or they don't get to the point, or they are rushing to finish their words.

  Our body, however, can only be in one place at a time. A grounding and centring exercise, even if just for a few minutes a day, trains you to be here now.

Grounding and centring

Find a comfortable position to stand with your feet slightly apart, hip width. Put your hands at your sides. Stand tall as if there was a string pulling you up so you stand tall but your chin is still parallel with the floor. Feel your feet being supported by the floor. Shift your body forward and backward, left and right, so your weight is in the centre. If needed, you can close your eyes as you breathe in and out slowly. With each breath, take note of how your abdomen moves. Take four or five breaths. If you need a little more time to feel fully present, take a few more breaths until you feel more present.

Here's an extended version of this exercise: When you feel more present, feel your body lengthening from your centre, three fingers below your navel. Visualise your feet going down to the ground, your legs and spine lengthening, and your head reaching up to the sky. Feel the extension of your length with each breath you take.

Next, experience your width from your centre. Feel your shoulders and your hips. Open your arms sideways as much as you can. Take up the space. Breathe in as you feel your width.

Now experience your depth. Feel yourself from front to back. Breathe in as your abdomen moves outward. Do you feel your back expand outward as well? Breathe out as your abdomen and back move inward. Feel your depth as you take a few more diaphragmatic breaths.

Lastly, bring your attention to feeling all of you, length, width, and depth. What are your sensations? Slowly open your eyes and write down your sensations and observations.

Follow the audio guidance with this exercise here:
http://developyourleadershipvoice.com/exercises

- Relaxation

  The best voice comes from the most relaxed body. So many clients have come to realise how much relaxation determines whether they can project their best voice. When they feel tension in their bodies, their voices are restricted. The importance of relaxation cannot be highlighted enough yet is also the most overlooked area.

  For professional athletes, relaxation is one of the contributors to peak performance. We don't tend to associate athletes with relaxation; stronger, higher, and faster would seem to describe the intensity of the training and pushing one's self to one's physical limits. It is proven that relaxation techniques, such as deep breathing exercises, meditation, visualisation, and progressive muscle relaxation, help athletes enhance focus during competition, manage anxiety and self-doubt, aid in muscle recovery, and reduce fatigue [7].

  In the chapter on space, we shared a relaxation exercise, "Body scan and relaxation," that you can practice on a regular basis. Diaphragmatic breathing is another way to help you relax. Even the "Grounding and centring" exercise can help you relax. When you're too busy to take time out to exercise properly, a sigh of relief could be just what you need.

Progressive muscle relaxation

Progressive muscle relaxation involves tensing and relaxing different muscle groups in the body to reduce tension and promote relaxation.

Find a comfortable place to stand. Breathe in through your mouth and hold your breath while you clench your fists and teeth, curl your toes, and tighten your neck muscles and the muscles in your groin. Hold this position and your breath for a count of five. Then stop clenching, relax all muscles, and exhale through your mouth. Repeat the exercise a few times to feel completely relaxed.

This exercise can also be practiced before important meetings and presentations when you feel nervous.

Follow the audio guidance for this exercise here:
http://developyourleadershipvoice.com/exercises

- Experiencing emotions fully

  Almost 20 years ago, I was pursuing my career in a foreign country. One night after work, I went to check out an apartment for rent. Disappointed with the apartment, I hopped on a bus to go home.

Sitting on the upper deck of the bus, I looked at the apartment buildings we passed, thinking to myself, "Where is my home?" I felt a heavy sensation in my chest. "No, no, no, I can't feel sad." My first reaction was to suppress it, having been educated that becoming emotional was not good. The more I tried to suppress it, the heavier my chest felt. So I gave up and allowed my body to experience the sensations, as tears streamed down my face. After some time, my chest started to feel lighter, and I sighed with relief, "Experiencing emotion can be such a relief!" Since then, I learned to stop suppressing my emotions and allow myself to experience my emotions fully.

In our society, emotions are often seen as barriers to efficiency and productivity. We suppress our emotions without being aware of the many health and psychological consequences, such as hypertension, heart disease, a weaker immune system, higher levels of anxiety and depression, and increased mortality risk, in addition to reduced social connection and support [8].

Experiencing emotions fully helps improve your physical health, reduces stress, improves communication, helps you make better decisions, builds resilience, and stimulates creativity. Of course, experiencing emotions fully does not mean taking it out on others. Take your own time in a private space to experience your emotions. There are many ways to help you release negative emotions, such as punching a pillow, axe throwing at an established venue, etc.

Speaking with emotion helps you cultivate your awareness and ability to express emotions. It leads you to a voice of equanimity. After all, equanimity is not about suppressing emotions but about experiencing them without being overwhelmed or controlled by them.

I AM ...

Equanimity is not a state that's easily attainable. It is a state, as well as a capacity, to allow us to move through life with grace, freedom, and wisdom. It requires ongoing self-development and advancement. When you are even halfway there, you will be a leader whom people look up to and turn to in times of uncertainty for assurance and inspiration.

One powerful way to help you cultivate equanimity and transform the way you project your voice is to shift what you identify yourself with.

"I don't belong"

May was in my group coaching program. She didn't speak up. She also didn't participate much in the first two sessions and gave the other participants the impression that she didn't want to stay in the group for long. In fact, she would often join the sessions late and leave early.

In one session, we talked about how your mental and emotional barriers could prevent you from projecting a powerful voice. She had an ah-ha moment, "Now I understand why! I always had the notion that I don't belong – everywhere I go and every group that I joined. As a result, I don't participate much and, indeed, people don't engage me much. This reinforces my belief that I don't belong!"

How we identify ourselves can lead us through a vicious cycle. Our sense of identity is the beliefs we hold about ourselves; for example, I don't belong. That belief guides our behaviours; if I believe I don't belong, my behaviours will reflect that belief; behaviours that may include not speaking up or participating much in a group setting or arriving late and leaving early. Our behaviours then elicit reactions out of others that reinforce our beliefs about ourselves; for example, because I don't participate, others don't include me, which reinforces your belief that you don't belong.

Following are some common inner beliefs that keep you from speaking with equanimity and a powerful voice.

- I don't belong.
  As just discussed, when you have this belief, you tend not to speak up or participate. When people don't include you, you don't feel seen or heard.

  To stop this vicious cycle, what identity belief could you adopt instead? It could be, "I belong to every group I'm in" or "I am welcomed everywhere I go." Write down the statements that resonate with you.

  Then live your life with this new identity. Act as if the new identity is who you are. When you join a new group, assume that everyone welcomes you and rejoices in your presence! With that assumption, how would you act differently?

- I don't matter.

  My opinions don't matter. What I say doesn't matter. These are variations of the same belief.

  All beliefs come from early childhood or significant life experiences. It is helpful to explore how this belief came about for you.

  This is a belief that I used to have. When I was growing up, my dad was domineering and I was always criticised and felt rejected. Over time, the little girl thought, "What's the point? Whatever I say makes no difference. Why even bother?"

  With this belief about yourself, you wouldn't speak up or fight for what you believe in because deep down you believe, "Whatever I say makes no difference. Why even bother?" People won't ask for your opinions because they may think you don't have one! Thus the vicious cycle: "I don't matter!"

  What could a new identity belief be? "I matter. I am important. My opinions contribute to the final decision. What I say makes a big difference."

  When you embrace this new identity belief, you'll start to speak up, argue constructively, and fight for what you believe in, and, as a result, people will start turning to you for suggestions and advice.
- I'm not good enough.

  This is a common belief that resonates with many people. Variations include "I'm not smart enough," "I don't know enough," "I'm not pretty enough," "I'm not experienced enough," "I'm not accomplished enough," "I'm not successful enough." You get the idea.

  Many clients who don't think they are good enough or know enough do not speak up or take a long time to form a sentence as they try to find the perfect word. As a result, they speak in broken sentences and they berate themselves for being so imperfect. And they can be very demanding of themselves.

  Where did this belief come from? Did you grow up in an environment where not being good enough was punished?

  What would your new identity belief be? "I'm good enough. Everything is perfect just the way it is. I know enough to support what I'm doing."

  You might wonder, "How can I improve if I think I'm good enough?" This goes back to the intention that we've talked about in the book. What's your intention for improvement? Is it from a place of lack? Is there something lacking in you that makes you less than? Or is it to help you work more efficiently or effectively?

There's a Japanese concept called *wabi-sabi*. If you accidentally break a vase, resulting in a long, jagged crack down the middle, your immediate reaction might be, "Oh, shoot, what a waste. I need to fix this or throw it away." With *wabi-sabi*, you would place the broken vase on a pedestal and honour the history and beauty of the imperfection by shining a spotlight on the crack, or you might see the crack as a branch and draw flowers around the crack. *Wabi-sabi* teaches us to embrace and appreciate our imperfections, seeing the hidden beauty right in front of our eyes and appreciating our own uniqueness.

- I'm not accepted.

  To compensate for feeling like you are not accepted, you may try to "fit in." As a result, you may not express what your true thoughts, or your opinions may vary, or you might sit on the fence. It's as if you don't have your own opinions.

  Deep down in the identify belief of not being accepted is "I'm not loved for who I am." Some people try to please others to be loved; some may work hard to achieve in order to be accepted, respected, and loved; some may avoid those who don't accept them and end up feeling lonely. What might the consequences of this identity belief be? And what upbringing and experiences have brought you to live with this identity?

  What new identity belief would you rather live with? "I am accepted everywhere I go. I was loved the moment I was born. I am loveable. I'm loved, no matter what. I'm loved, without having to do anything to prove it. I'm loved for who I am. I am love."

What are your identity barriers? How have these barriers created the vicious cycles? What will your new identity beliefs be? Act as if they were true and they will become true.

Isn't it interesting to think about our beliefs and how they came about? We were born perfect and whole. Then we started to adopt all the human nonsense and became so broken. Hopefully, one day it will dawn on you that it is time to heal the broken parts so you become whole again. That is what we are here to do as human beings – at least, that is one of our purposes.

REFERENCES

[1] Davidson, R. J., and Begley, S. (2012). *The Emotional Life of Your Brain: How Its Unique Patterns Affect the Way You Think, Feel, and Live – And How You Can Change Them*. New York: Hudson Street Press.

[2] Kabat-Zinn, J. (1990). *Full Catastrophe Living: Using the Wisdom of Your Body and Mind to Face Stress, Pain, and Illness*. New York: Dell.

[3] Hölzel, B. K., Carmody, J., Vangel, M., Congleton, C., Yerramsetti, S. M., et al. (2011). "Mindfulness Practice Leads to Increases in Regional Brain Gray Matter Density." *Psychiatry Research: Neuroimaging*, 191(1), 36–43.

[4] Lutz, A., Slagter, H. A., Dunne, J. D., and Davidson, R. J. (2008). "Attention Regulation through Synchrony Training: A Study of Long-Term Meditators." *PLOS One*, 3(4), e1897.

[5] Porges, S. W. (2011). *The Polyvagal Theory: Neurophysiological Foundations of Emotions, Attachment, Communication, and Self-Regulation*. New York: W. W. Norton & Company.

[6] Ma, X., Yue, Z. Q., Gong, Q. Y., Zhang, R., Duan, N., et al. (2017). "The Effect of Diaphragmatic Breathing on Attention, Negative Affect and Stress in Healthy Adults." *Frontiers in Psychology*, 8, 874.

[7] Parnabas, V., Mahamood, Y., Parnabas, J., and Nazarudin, M. N. (2014). "The Relationship between Relaxation Techniques and Sport Performance." *Universal Journal of Psychology*, 2(3), 108–112.

[8] Chapman, B. P., Fiscella, K., Kawachi, I., Duberstein, P., and Muennig, P. (2013). "Emotion Suppression and Mortality Risk over a 12-Year Follow-Up." *Journal of Psychosomatic Research*, 75(2), 149–153.

Seven

"Infinite patience brings immediate results."

– *Wayne Dyer*

In over 15 years of helping clients from all over the world to speak with a powerful voice, I've noticed that some clients would take a much longer time to see transformations in their voices than others, while a small handful of clients would take less than the average duration of 6 months to see the transformation. When the skills and processes are the same, what made the difference?

WHAT'S HOLDING YOU BACK?

"How could it be possible?"

Sharon's voice sounded young and people wouldn't associate her with a senior position in her company had they met her for the first time. People would take quite some time to get to know her before they realised she was experienced and competent. So Sharon wanted to develop a voice that projected more maturity and authority.

In the first session, she asked, "Is it really possible to change my voice?" I showed her the videos of clients who had transformed their voices and explained how the voice worked and how it could be changed.

Halfway through the second session, she asked as we were practicing breathing exercises, "Is it possible at all to change the breathing? I've been breathing in the wrong way for years!" So I explained to her how the breathing worked and where the potential for change was for her.

During the third session – no surprise – she asked again, "How could it be possible to change the voice? I've been speaking in this way all my life."

DOI: 10.4324/9781003596486-7

I laughed, "Did you notice that you asked if it was possible at all to change your voice in EVERY session? If you have one foot on the gas and the other foot on the brake, how are you going to move forward?"

"Yeah," Sharon sighed. "We'll have to work on that belief. If not, you'll not be able to make progress."

That's one of the reasons why some clients were not able to make progress as quickly as they expected – and so they remained – stagnant. On the one hand, you can have a strong desire to make a change; on the other hand, there is an underlying hesitation or fear that prevents you from making a full commitment. It could be a fear of failure or a fear of the unknown.

Another common block some clients have is wondering, "Can I achieve it?"

"Do you have a few brain cells less than the other clients?" I often joke with them. "If not, then why is it that they could achieve a powerful voice and you can't?"

When doubts arise, we normally break down the skills and processes into smaller and achievable steps so the clients can make progress incrementally and gain confidence and momentum.

"I don't have time to practice," or "I'm too busy to practice," many clients have said. We are living in a society where being busy seems to be a good thing, and people equate that to being successful. Being busy leads to a decrease in productivity and efficiency and an increase in mental and physical health risks. As American football coach John Wooden put it, "Never mistake activity for achievement." If it's a priority for you, you'll find the time.

I was surprised to observe the lack of resourcefulness in some clients who are senior-level leaders. When they hit a wall in their practices, their first reaction is, "This doesn't work for me." People who are resourceful might instead think, "If it has worked for others, how can I make it work for me?" Resourcefulness is the difference between someone who make things happen and someone who keeps hoping for new and interesting tactics. "If you can't get through it, dig a hole under it." That is resourcefulness.

Be like bamboo

"So if I do this breathing exercise, I'll get a powerful voice, right?" Kevin asked in the first two coaching sessions.

"We wish that was how voice transformation works." I laughed. "Transformation is not linear. It's not like, if you plant a seed, you'll get fruits. There is so much complexity at play with both internal and external factors. Do you know how many years a bamboo seed takes for its shoot to emerge above the ground?" I asked.

"No idea," Kevin replied.

"That's an expected answer. Most people have no idea!" I shared, "It can take 3 to 5 years. That means, for the first 3 years, NOTHING – literally nothing – grows out of the soil. Many people would give up if they saw nothing. What happens underneath the ground is that bamboo is developing a strong root system, a robust foundation. That's why bamboo is so resilient and can stand so much in a storm. And that's why the bamboo is so strong that it was used to build houses in China for centuries. Once bamboo shoots emerge from the ground, bamboo grows like crazy, up to 91 cm [36 inches] per day!"

"Hats off to the bamboos!" Kevin laughed.

"It's the same for the voice." I continued, "The good news is that you don't need 3 to 5 years! Phew. Breathing is only the first step."

"I see," Kevin said. "Let's get to work!"

A linear thinking pattern is a common block for many clients in their voice transformation process: "If I do A and I'll get B." This can be misleading and damaging.

If you do A and don't get B, many people become frustrated and start to question their capability and competence.

If you do A and don't get B, many people think perhaps it's because they aren't trying hard enough. So they keep trying the wrong things and hearing the same banal phrases: "Never give up," or "Persevere until you succeed," or "Be resilient."

Change is not linear. Growth is not linear. Life is not linear.

The voice transformation process is very much like the process of growing a seed. Water the seed. Give it sunshine, maybe even fertiliser. You'll see the sprouts grow faster than you expect.

THE LAW OF LEAST EFFORT

Have fun!

Ron shared his frustration during one session about his practice on developing an engaging voice that piques the audience's curiosity. "I was not born for this. I've tried so hard and practiced every day without much progress."

I laughed, "That's where the problem is!"

He looked confused.

I continued, "Remember, I said to have fun with this practice! You are trying so hard. That's not the way. Developing your engaging voice is a relaxed and fun process. You are treating it too seriously."

"Yes, that has always been my style."

"Have fun!" I reinforced. "You are intelligent enough to know that change does not happen immediately, let alone your old habits and style! See this practice as an experiment. We are trying things out and we'll see how it goes! If it doesn't work, we'll try something else to make it work."

"Phew!" Ron sighed. "Now I feel more relieved."

When things are not working, most people think they need to work harder to make things happen. It's not only Ron who was dealing with this misconception. Most people think the same way and live their lives in the same manner, a stubborn mindset developed in our societies.

Nothing in nature tries hard to achieve a certain result. Rivers never try hard to run to the ocean; they follow the path of least resistance. Seeds don't try hard to sprout; they come out of the soil effortlessly. Embryos don't try hard to become a baby; they follow nature's programming. Nature functions on a path of least resistance. When we learn from nature and apply the law of least resistance, we achieve what we want: "do less and achieve more."

No, this doesn't mean that you will do nothing and wait for the results to come to you. In fact, you ARE going to make an effort and work hard but align your intention, goals, and actions with the natural flow of things, rather than resisting, forcing, or struggling against it. For example, I was shocked to discover that many people around me have undergone cosmetic procedures and even plastic surgery procedures to defy ageing or enhance their physical appearance. Though there are many different opinions on this, I don't believe it aligns with the natural flow of things. It can come from a place of insecurity, from societal pressure, or from the belief that outer beauty will solve the inner issues. The negative consequences of cosmetic and plastic surgery procedures are long-lasting. Following the law of least resistance, you can work out regularly, pay attention to your diet, and most importantly, continuously evolve mentally, emotionally, and spiritually so you can age gracefully.

What made you choose your career? Is it because that's where the money is, or is it because that's what you love to do or, even better, that's what helps you to fulfil your purpose? The latter two reasons align with the law of least resistance. The saying, "Do what you love and the money will follow" is true. "Do what you love and you'll never work a day in your life." Of course, you'll have to put forth effort and work hard, but the result will come more easily without the struggle!

As leaders, if you want people to respect you, trust you, and follow you, according to the law of least resistance, this means caring about people, listening to their challenges and needs, having their best interest in mind, and nurturing and empowering them, not making unnecessary rules to limit them, which will most likely lead to rebellion; not micromanaging people, which will result in a lack of trust, responsibility, or creativity. Lao Tzu stated, "无为而无所不为" and "无为而治." The literal translation is, "Doing nothing to achieve everything" and "Doing nothing to lead [a country]." The latter is where Lao Tzu brought this concept up in the first place, the philosophy of leading a country. It is not to do nothing but to do things or set up regulations to help care for, nurture, and empower people, instead of limiting, restricting, or micromanaging them.

"If I died tomorrow …"

When I started my career as a voice coach and professional speaker 15 years ago, I heard experienced speakers say, "As a speaker, one must write a book." So I started to prepare to write a book just a few months after I started my new career. As a newbie in the market, I didn't think any established publisher would publish my future book.

So I talked with a local self-publisher, who told me the minimum figure for self-publishing with him was over five figures! I didn't want to invest that much. And thinking of all the work I would have to do gave me a headache. After writing two and a half chapters, I didn't feel motivated to write anymore.

Four years later, one night as I walked back home from a full-day workshop, a thought came to me: "Oh my God, if I died tomorrow, all the things I know about voice would die with me! I'd better write a book!"

I remembered I had met someone from a publishing company who was a panelist in a conference I'd attended a year ago. "What is his name?" I went online to the conference website. Luckily, they still kept the information from last year's conference! I contacted the person from the publishing company and shared my idea about the book. Then I had one meeting with two members of his team and the rest is history.

"What? That easy?" Whenever I shared how I got an established publisher to publish my first book, many fellow speakers thought it was unbelievable. Yes, it was that easy. I wish I could have had a more motivational story for you where I struggled to find a publisher after being rejected 50 times! But no one wants to struggle that much. There IS an easier way, to do less and achieve more when you align your intention and action with how things naturally flow.

And if you haven't read that first book of mine, *Influence Through Voice*, check it out on my website: https://powerfulexecutivevoice.com/shop

You've heard me say more than once throughout this book that the best voice comes from the most relaxed body. Developing proper voice projection is indeed a process with the least effort. The more relaxed you are, the more freely your voice is projected. The less effort you use – in fact, zero effort – the stronger your voice will be. This sounds counter-intuitive. Voice projection does not use effort. Speaking is relaxing and releasing of tension and toxins. Remember that voice is projected on the out breath. Speaking is supposed to be enjoyable as you release the tension and toxins out of your body as you breathe out. Many clients have frowned upon hearing this: "I wish I could feel that. But now all I'm feeling is tension and stress, especially in front of a group in high-stake situations."

Now sigh a few times. Did you use effort when you sighed? No. If you did, you weren't sighing correctly! Sighing is exactly how you should feel whenever you speak. It is relaxation and relief.

To use the least effort while achieving the strongest sound, what you need to do is to create a conducive environment in your body for the best sound to come out. What is this conducive environment? It is a relaxed body with all the resonating chambers active and available to produce sound. To create this conducive environment, you need to breathe properly with the support of your diaphragm, activate the chest cavity, and develop full resonance. Most of all, relax at all times and make these three steps a habit. When the conducive environment is created, the result – an effortlessly powerful voice – will come.

The biggest mistake many clients make is going against the law of least effort. That is, they take the short cut of purposely lowering their voice by pressing their vocal cords down. When you do that, you interrupt the natural flow of how voice works. In addition to your voice sounding unclear and not projecting far, you can damage your vocal cords. This instant gratification only provides short-lived results.

In today's world, unfortunately, most people want instant gratification and have no patience for a solid process that'll bring lasting results. They look at the short-term gain without considering the long-term consequences. This is like popping pills to eliminate pain in the body. Yes, Western medicine can ease pain while causing damage due to their many side effects.

You need to look at developing your full voice from a wholesome perspective. Don't just press your vocal cords to get a temporary low-pitched voice. Take your time to form habits with proper diaphragmatic breathing and full resonance; the results will last and benefit you in so many other areas, as discussed in the chapter on gravitas. Have patience with the process of forming habits. Then your powerful voice will always be ready for you to use, at any time, especially when you are nervous or stressed, because it will become second nature. Infinite patience does bring immediate results.

LETTING GO

It may seem that the voice transformation process is philosophical; this is correct, but it is still more of a practical process. The perspectives presented in this book will help you transform your voice using the right mindset and approach, which will save you half the struggle, if there is struggle at all.

Just as everything in life is a practice of mindfulness, so is the voice transformation process. Mindfulness is a concept that has gained popularity in the business world in recent years. It is a practice of being fully present and engaged in the moment, acknowledging and accepting your feelings, thoughts, and bodily sensations without judgement. It helps improve your physical, mental, and emotional well-being and better manage stress in a busy world.

Overwhelming stress can take a toll on the way we breathe and the way we use our breath in voice projection. Not breathing properly is a default for most people. Some clients note that they stop breathing when they feel stressed out, and most do not use their breath properly in voice projection. Holding the breath is one of the most common mistakes. Breath reflects how we interact with people and the world around us. When we are stressed out and in fight-or-flight mode, we tend to grasp onto things to feel a sense of being in control. This results in breath-holding while speaking, followed by breathlessness. The more tightly we grasp, the greater the pressure is building up inside of us, which can lead to burnout and health problems.

A simple practice, though it may not be easy to apply, is to breathe out when speaking. Voice is produced when you breathe out. Instead of holding your breath, let go of your breath while speaking.

How often do you pay attention to your breath while speaking? Probably only when you feel like you are running out of breath or do not have enough breath to sustain your speech.

A new habit you want to form is breathing out when you speak. You can start by using more breath on key words – the words that help convey your message – which are also the words that you want people to remember. We talked about this in previous chapters, and it is worth re-iterating.

Letting go of the breath

Let's try the following sentences:

"The best voice comes from the most relaxed body. You must breathe out when you speak."

The key words are "best," "most," and "must." So you will breathe out more on these words. After speaking these words, you should be prompted automatically to inhale so you'll always have enough breath to sustain your speech.

Let's indicate the exhalation (on key words, which are in bold) and inhalation points for the sentences:

[Inhale] The **best** voice [inhale] comes from the **most** [inhale] relaxed body. [inhale] You **must** [inhale] breathe out when you speak.

You may also notice that you automatically slowed down on those words.

The second inhalation is after the word "voice" instead of "best" because "best voice" is a short phrase and the inhalation happens more naturally there. There is no right or wrong. You can try it and see where it sounds natural for you.

We indicate the inhalation points to show you how often you need to inhale. However, your focus is NOT on where you should inhale but on where you should exhale more. When you exhale all your breath on the key words, you will automatically be prompted to inhale. If you are not prompted, then you are not using all your breath on the key words. When you are speaking, you don't want to be distracted by too many things to focus on, such as when you should inhale, when you should exhale more, what your message is, etc. Focus on one thing; that is, using more breath on key words. The rest will take care of itself. Learn to let go of trying to control every single aspect.

A demonstration of this exercise can be found here:

http://developyourleadershipvoice.com/exercises

"I believe there are stones growing in my kidney"

Linda seemed to have done her research before working with me on her voice, trying to sound more mature and authoritative, "I have worked on breathing before. And we can skip the breathing and go to the next step. These are the different exercises I have found. Let's do these exercises."

I laughed. "Sometimes I feel like a doctor. It's like going to a surgeon and saying, 'I have pain on the side of my body. I have self-diagnosed as kidney issues. I believe there are stones growing in my kidney. You are going to help me remove the stones. Let's now perform the surgery.' I can't do anything before I give you a full diagnosis, including scanning to see whether you have stones in your kidney at all."

"Voice work may look simple, with just a few steps, but that's because I have made it simple after years of trial and error working on myself first, followed by hundreds of cases with clients." I continued, "Even if you have worked on breathing, we'll need to see whether you are doing diaphragmatic breathing at all and whether it's a habit."

Indeed, diaphragmatic breathing had not become a habit for Linda. Based on her previous breathing practices, I designed two exercises for her so it would become a habit more quickly.

We also discovered that she needed to expand her lung capacity so she wouldn't run out of breath so easily. We discovered that her body was extremely tense. We needed some time to help her relax, especially when it came to practising the step on activating the chest cavity to prepare for resonance. What's even more important was that she needed to let go of control, both in how she was holding the breath and in how she needed to allow the body to take over, instead of using the mind to control how the body should work. She needed more work than she had thought.

This is another example of trying to stay in control. It is understandable that when you are experiencing a serious problem you want to be on top of things. You are not a doctor, after all. Let the professionals do their jobs. Let go of control on how things should go.

Another common issue is the tendency to use the mind to control how the body should work. We talked about this in the chapter on space. For example, when we breathe out properly, the abdomen should move inward; when we breathe in, the abdomen should move outward. Instead of allowing this to happen naturally, many clients who are more analytical and technical wind up performing unsynchronised movement; that is, their abdomen moves inward followed by an exhalation. This unsynchronised movement looks so funny. When I point this out, they often realise they are trying to use their mind to control how their body works. This is the same problem we discussed regarding activation and full resonance practices in the chapter on gravitas. Let go of your mind. Trust that your body knows how to work. All you need to do is to let the abdomen move inward when breathing out; the rest will happen naturally.

One key element in letting go is trust: trusting the process, that when you plant a seed, followed by essential steps such as watering, providing sunlight, etc., it will grow out of the soil. If it doesn't, you need to determine what the problem is and solve it. It might be that the seed is damaged, or you watered too much, or it was exposed to too much sunlight.

But the process is correct: a healthy seed will grow out of the soil with the appropriate amount of water, sunlight, etc.

GETTING WORSE BEFORE GETTING BETTER

Sometimes things have to get worse before they get better.

The transformation process is a detox process in which everything that needs to leave our system must first come up. That which lies unconsciously within us comes up for review so that we might consciously see where we are blocked and then be able to remove these blocks.

It's very much like the evolution of a romantic relationship. The beginning of a courtship is a bed of roses and both people are wearing rose-colored glasses. As the couple gets to know each other more and become more intimate, conflicts will inevitably come up. It can often seem that things are getting worse the longer you are together. But it is the conflicts that show how well we can deal with the other person's habits and patterns, where inside of ourselves we have never looked at and worked on, what our blind spots are, etc. These issues come to the forefront for review, so both individuals can assess whether they want to and can address them. If they are willing and able to, they will work through the conflicts and grow closer, ultimately strengthening and sustaining the relationship.

In your voice transformation process, sometimes it may seem that you are not getting the exercises right and the more you practice, the worse it becomes. Most clients begin to doubt that they are making process at all or whether they are cut out to speak with a powerful voice. Remember that things have to become worse before they get better. In the voice transformation process, stuff has to come up first for review before you can make progress. For example, are you more analytical, involved in the details, or do you have the tendency to want to be in control and have a hard time letting go? Do you approach learning in a linear or non-linear fashion? Do you use your head intelligence more, your body intelligence more, or your heart intelligence more, as discussed in the previous chapter? What might be stopping you mentally and emotionally, that is, the fear of visibility, the fear of being judged, the tendency to please or fit in? Transformation is indeed not a linear process. Step A does not straightforwardly lead to result B. A lot can come up that you will need to examine and work through.

The voice transformation process is holistic and wholesome. Keep an open mind and be prepared for spiral growth. Stay flexible and be resourceful. Adapt and stay committed. When you emerge from the other side, you'll feel so fulfilled that not only will your voice be transformed but you will have evolved and been elevated to a much higher level than expected.

CONCLUSION

As a shy and timid fresh graduate who was bullied and unheard, I went on a journey to become more assertive. In my pursuit of assertiveness, I was fortunate to stumble upon the study of the speaking voice that has changed my life and the lives of people around the world. My powerful voice has led me to speak on five continents and enabled me to be respected by audiences and clients from around the world and seen as a person of influence. Over the years, I've come to realise that I was chosen to do this work. Empowering you to speak with a powerful voice is my purpose and mission in life.

The power in your voice is beyond measure. Most people have only scratched the surface of voice work. When you can commit yourself to the deep dive of voice work, you will start to notice that people will look up to you, come to you for reassurance and advice when they are lost in uncertainty, and gather around you for motivation and inspiration. That's where you fulfil your purpose and mission in life.

Here's my wish for you:

May you clear the cloud over you so you can see clearly who you are.
May you accept, embrace, and love who you are.
May you be guided to stay grounded and centred with who you are.
May you lead from compassion towards others as well as yourself.
May you become the pillar of strength that people are looking for in the midst of the storm.
May you speak with a powerful voice and leave a mark on the world.

Index

For Product Safety Concerns and Information please contact our EU representative GPSR@taylorandfrancis.com Taylor & Francis Verlag GmbH, Kaufingerstraße 24, 80331 München, Germany